B1–B2

intermediate to upper-intermediate

Business Impact 1.1

Modules A, B and C

Stephanie Ashford
Louis Rogers
Jason Humphreys
Robert Kirstein

Access all the accompanying digital components for this book on **allango**, the DELTA Publishing language learning platform:

Scan the QR code or go directly to **www.allango.co.uk**

Enter this licence key to activate the additional components:

EKS-501070-414e-3b2c-71fb

When you see this symbol, accompanying digital content is available.

DELTA Publishing

Authors Stephanie Ashford, Louis Rogers, Jason Humphreys, Robert Kirstein
Managing editor Helge Sturmfels
Editor Gillian Bathmaker
Layout and typesetting Anne-Katrin Enderlein, büro freilich
Cover picture Getty Images (LightFieldStudios), München
Cover Silke Wewoda

The authors and the publisher would like to thank everyone who contributed to the successful completion of this project.

Information and additional products / material for this series can be found here:
www.deltapublishing.co.uk/business-impact

1. edition 1 3 2 1 | 2026 25 24
The last figure shown denotes the year of impression.

DELTA Publishing, an imprint of the Ernst Klett Sprachen GmbH

www.deltapublishing.co.uk
www.klett-sprachen.de/delta

Printing and binding Elanders Waiblingen GmbH

ISBN 978-3-12-501070-3

9 783125 010703

Business Impact

This innovative modular business English course covers two levels B1-B2 (intermediate to upper-intermediate) and B2-C1 (upper-intermediate to advanced) in six books (print + digital). Each of the six books comprises three modules, A, B and C. All modules are also available as stand-alone digital modules.

All **A Modules** have a strong focus on **personal encounters,** all **B Modules** focus primarily on **day-to-day business** and all **C Modules** focus on **business results.**

Modules can be chosen individually to suit the level, interests and requirements of classes, allowing full flexibility and control in terms of content and progress.

Welcome to **Business Impact 1.1**
Module A

Business Impact 1.1.A is the A Module from *Business Impact 1.1.* This module focuses on **personal encounters in the business world** and will help you master meetings and greetings in business situations.

The page numbers on this page refer to the printed edition of Business Impact 1.1.

Business Impact

This innovative modular business English course covers two levels B1-B2 (intermediate to upper-intermediate) and B2-C1 (upper-intermediate to advanced) in six books (print + digital). Each of the six books comprises three modules, A, B and C. All modules are also available as stand-alone digital modules.

All **A Modules** have a strong focus on **personal encounters,** all **B Modules** focus primarily on **day-to-day business** and all **C Modules** focus on **business results.**

Modules can be chosen individually to suit the level, interests and requirements of classes, allowing full flexibility and control in terms of content and progress.

Welcome to **Business Impact 1.1 Module B**

Business Impact 1.1.B is the B Module from *Business Impact 1.1.* This module focuses on **day-to-day business** and will help you master the organisation and carrying out of business meetings.

The page numbers on this page refer to the printed edition of Business Impact 1.1.

Business Impact

This innovative modular business English course covers two levels B1-B2 (intermediate to upper-intermediate) and B2-C1 (upper-intermediate to advanced) in six books (print + digital). Each of the six books comprises three modules, A, B and C. All modules are also available as stand-alone digital modules.

All **A Modules** have a strong focus on **personal encounters,** all **B Modules** focus primarily on **day-to-day business** and all **C Modules** focus on **business results.**

Modules can be chosen individually to suit the level, interests and requirements of classes, allowing full flexibility and control in terms of content and progress.

Welcome to **Business Impact 1.1**
Module C

Business Impact 1.1.C is the C Module from *Business Impact 1.1*. This module focuses on **business results** and will help you become proficient in dealings with numbers & figures and goals & plans.

The page numbers on this page refer to the printed edition of Business Impact 1.1.

Agenda

- Greetings & small talk
- Addressing clients & colleagues
- Names & titles
- First contacts

Greeting *new colleagues*

› to give someone a high five | to press your hands together | to give a *namaste* (to someone) | to shake hands (with someone) | to bow (to someone) (Tip: 'bow' rhymes with 'how') | to hug (a person) | to take a person in your arms | to kiss a person on the cheek ‹

› Small talk

Start the session by chatting with a partner about the current weather for a few minutes. Your conversation can, of course, move on to other topics that come up naturally. Use the following phrases in your conversation.

I know exactly what you mean!

Oh, my goodness!

Tip

A quick chat at the beginning of every English class is a great opportunity to practise and improve your small talk skills.

› Down to business

1 Discuss the following questions in class.

1. Which of the ways of greeting people shown in the photos above have you experienced in a business or private context? Which have you never experienced?
2. What other ways of greeting people in a business context do you know, or have you experienced?
3. How do you and your colleagues usually greet each other (at different times of day)?
4. How do you usually greet English-speaking visitors?

› p. 4 in digital module 1.1.A

A.01 **2a** **A visitor has arrived at reception in your company. Listen and find the badge offered (X) and the right badge for the visitor (✓).**

2b **Talk in class: Have you ever made a mistake addressing people? How did you deal with the situation?**

3a **Look at the forms of address below. Match each one to its correct usage (status, gender and context).**

Form of address		Usage (status, gender, context)
1. Ms	☐	a) a man, marital status not relevant
2. Mr	☐	b) in written correspondence (email / letter) if the name is not known
3. Mrs		
4. Miss	☐	c) formal and polite way of speaking to a man
5. Mx	☐	d) formal and polite way of speaking to a woman
6. Dr	☐	e) in an email or letter where the name is known
7. Dear Sir or Madam	☐	f) woman, marital status not relevant
8. Dear Mr Jones	☐	g) informal greeting, gender neutral
9. Ma'am, madam	☐	h) gender and marital status not relevant
10. Sir	☐	i) addressing members of an audience when giving a speech
11. Hi (+ first name)	☐	j) a single woman
12. Ladies and gentlemen	☐	k) a doctor (medical or academic)
	☐	l) a married woman

3b **Look at the following guidelines for using titles in English. Read them and then discuss whether the same guidelines apply in your language.**

Business Impact

1 If you're not sure of the gender, use the name without the title.
2 Using 'Mrs' and 'Miss' is becoming less common.
3 'Mx' and 'Ms' are normally written, not spoken.
4 One title is enough, e.g. Professor Jones or Dr Jones, not Mr Professor Jones or Mr Dr Jones.
5 Users of American English are more likely to add a full-stop after the title, e.g. Mr. Jones.

› p. 5 in digital module 1.1.A

4 **Practise in pairs. Create a visitor's badge for your partner.**

1. Ask your partner appropriate questions and complete the details for his / her badge.
2. When you've finished, ask your partner to check the details.
3. Change partners and practise again.

Visitor 1

Visitor 2

ENERGIZER

Enjoy watching this video clip.

▶ A.1

5 **Small talk: Many people introduce themselves by their first name, or soon switch to first name terms. What's the policy in your organisation? Chat with a partner and exchange your ideas.**

6a **Look at the names below and discuss the questions in class.**

1. How do you think the names are pronounced?
2. Do you think the name is typically male (M), female (F), or gender-neutral (N)?
3. Which of the names do you think is the first name and which is the surname?

Tip

To check if a name is male or female, a surname or a first name, or how to pronounce a name, enter the name in a search engine and add, for example, "first" name or "surname".

Ghislaine Guillaume

Phoenix Constantine

Siobhan Coughlan

Nguyễn Xuân Phúc

A.02-05 **6b** **Now listen. Underline the person's surname and add the additional information.**

1. **Ghislaine Guillaume**
   M ☐ F ☐ N ☐
   Title (if known): ____________
   Preferred form of address: ____________

2. **Siobhan Coughlan**
   M ☐ F ☐ N ☐
   Title (if known): ____________
   Preferred form of address: ____________

3. **Phoenix Constantine**
   M ☐ F ☐ N ☐
   Title (if known): ____________
   Preferred form of address: ____________

4. **Nguyễn Xuân Phúc**
   M ☐ F ☐ N ☐
   Title (if known): ____________
   Preferred form of address: ____________

6c **What would you say in the following situations? Suggest suitable phrases, then listen again to check.**

1. You're greeting someone face-to-face for the first time. Pleased to meet you!
2. You're not sure you heard the name properly.
3. You'd like the person to address you in a certain way, e.g. by using your first name.
4. You want to check how to say the person's name.
5. You'd like to ask someone how they prefer to be addressed.
6. You want to apologise to a person for making a mistake with their name.
7. You want to tell someone you don't know how to say their name.

7 **Practise with different partners: Have a short conversation introducing yourselves and establishing how to address each other. Practise using phrases you noted down in 6c in your conversation.**

› Review and AOB

Review what you have learned in this session:

1. Suggest three ways in which people in different parts of the world greet each other.
2. Explain when to use the terms Ms, Mrs and Mx.
3. Suggest a phrase you can use to confirm whether to address a person by their first or last name.
4. Suggest a fairly formal greeting for when you meet someone face-to-face for the first time.

› Final feedback

What did you find most useful in this session? Tell the class. Any questions?

1 **Read the following article about mistaken identities.**

Business Impact

HOW *embarrassing!*

Making a mistake about a business partner's name or identity shouldn't happen – but sometimes it does! While it can be very embarrassing at the time, it's often funny in retrospect. Here are some classic examples.

Mr or Mrs?

The most embarrassing thing happened to me a few years ago! I had to call a client to apologise for a wrong delivery. When he answered the phone, he seemed surprised to hear from me, but was more than happy to accept a refund. We ended up having a really nice chat about all sorts of things, including his new project and his dog - a poodle called Fluffy. I ended the call by asking "Is there anything else I can do for you, Mr Fabricious?". There was an awkward silence, then the person at the other end of the line said, "Actually, I'm Mrs Fabricious. I just have a very deep voice.". Luckily, she was very nice about it. Apparently, I wasn't the first person to make the same mistake. ***Jodie***

Just a joke?

I was at a job interview and the secretary met me at the reception. She took me to the interview room and told me to wait outside because I was early. So, I gave her my coat and asked her to get me a coffee with two sugars "and a double vodka to calm my nerves!". She didn't smile. She just gave me a funny look. Anyway, a few minutes later, she came back with my coffee and led me into the interview room. She invited me to take a seat, sat down next to one of the interviewers, and introduced herself as a member of the works council! ***Franco***

A broken man

I was having a meeting with an important client in Italy when there was a loud buzzing sound. My client threw her arms up in the air, cried what sounded to me like "Signor Rotto", went downstairs and came back with a visitor, one of her colleagues. We shook hands and I said "Pleased to meet you, Signor Rotto.". He looked confused, then my client explained that before she left the room she had said "il citofono è rotto", which is Italian for "the intercom is broken". She and Signor Rotto tried to keep a straight face after that, but they kept cracking up. ***Isaac***

Magazine

2 **Explain the mistake that each of the people made in your own words.**

3 **Expand your vocabulary: Find the phrases in the article. (The paragraph numbers are in brackets.) Then choose (✓) the best meaning for the words in bold in the context of the anecdotes.**

Phrase	Option 1	Option 2	Option 3
it's often **funny** (1)	odd	strange	comical
in retrospect (1)	on second thoughts	looking back	on review
classic examples (1)	typical	traditional	simple
more than **happy** to do something (2)	satisfied	willing	lucky
an **awkward** silence (2)	clumsy	stiff	embarrassing
Apparently … (2)	Clearly	Seemingly	Possibly
keep a **straight** face (4)	serious	upright	honest

4 **An online thesaurus can help you find new ways to express things. Look up the words in bold in an online thesaurus. (The paragraph numbers are in brackets.) Which options do you find? Which is the most appropriate in the context of the anecdotes?**

Tip
Enter "online thesaurus English" into a search engine to find an online thesaurus.

	Best option	Alternative 1	Alternative 2
to be very **nice** about it (2)	*kind*	*friendly*	*fair*
a **funny** look (3)			
classic examples (1)			
to **cry** (4)			
to look **confused** (4)			
to **crack up** (4)			

5 **Optional extra: Have you or anyone you know ever made a similar mistake in identity? Prepare a short anecdote to present in the next session. Try to include words and phrases from tasks 3 and 4 where possible.**

Agenda
- Job titles
- Describing your job
- Getting tenses right

Job *talk*

› Small talk

Start the session by chatting with a partner about your current work situation for a few minutes. Your conversation can, of course, move on to other topics that come up naturally. Use the phrases on the right in your conversation.

Oh, really? Why's that?

That sounds familiar!

› Down to business

1 Discuss the following questions in class.

1. The same job title was given as the search word for each of the photos above. What job title do you think it was?
2. What kind of image would you choose to illustrate your job? Why?

› p. 10 in digital module 1.1.A

2a **Look at the categories 1 - 5 below. What do you think the jobs might be? Collect ideas in class for three or more jobs for each category.**

1 Highest-paid jobs
2 Fastest-growing jobs globally
3 Lowest-paid jobs
4 Jobs people most want
5 Highest-paid jobs in business

2b **Look at the lists of jobs below. Ask and answer the following questions first with a partner, then in class.**

Which job / jobs in the lists …
1. … have you never heard of before?
2. … are there in your organisation?
3. … is / are closest to your job?
4. … is a job you'd like to do?
5. … is a job you'd never want to do?

List A
- Pilot
- Writer
- Dancer
- YouTuber
- Entrepreneur

List B
- Chief Executive Officer (CEO)
- Chief Financial Officer (CFO)
- Investment banker
- Management consultant
- Marketing director
- IT director

List C
- AI and machine learning specialist
- Information security analyst
- Robotics engineer
- Agriculture equipment operator
- Scaffolder

List D
- Farm labourer
- Domestic worker
- Street vendor
- Fast food worker
- Call centre operator

List E
- Medical specialist: cardiologist, surgeon, dermatologist, radiologist, anaesthetist, dentist
- Athlete / sports competitor
- Chief executive
- Airline pilot
- Lawyer

Tip
Use an online dictionary to find the meanings of any jobs that are new for you.

ENERGIZER
Enjoy watching this video clip.
A.2

2c **Match the lists A - E to the categories 1 - 5 in task 2a. Which jobs do you think will or will not still be in the same categories in 10 years' time?**

3a You are at an international conference. Before the next session starts you make small talk about your job with another delegate. What would you expect to find out about the other person in the first few minutes?

A.06 **3b** Listen to three people at the international conference making small talk about their jobs. Did you find out the things you expected? What else did you find out about each person and their job?

4a Focus on tenses: The following sentences 1 - 4 are all from the audio. Match each one to its function.

Sentence	Function
1. I **build up** and **sustain** strong relationships with my clients.	☐ a) Describes a current activity.
2. Right now I'**m looking for** potential new clients.	☐ b) Describes a regular activity.
3. I'**ve worked / been working** in HR since I left college.	☐ c) Describes an activity from a time that is now past.
4. Then I **worked** as a personnel manager.	☐ d) Describes an activity that started at some point in the past and is still ongoing.

4b Which tense is used for each function? Add the sentence number.

☐ **simple present**
☐ **present perfect (progressive)**
☐ **present progressive**
☐ **simple past**

4c The following sentences are also from the audio. Consider the functions and complete the sentences using the verbs below in the correct tense.

› be | decide | develop | give | join | manage | oversee | provide | start | think | try | work ‹

Describing what you do on a regular basis.

1. I ______________________________ a team of 16 people.
2. We ______________________________ technical support.
3. I ______________________________ data security.

Describing what you are currently doing.

4. At the moment we ______________________________ a new cybersecurity system.
5. We ______________________________ to attract nurses who have retired.
6. If you ______________________________ of coming back to nursing, give me a call.

Talking about things that are still ongoing, but started in the past.

7. I ______________________________ always ______________________________ interested in wine.
8. We ______________________________ just ______________________________ a major recruitment drive.
9. How long ______________________________ you ______________________________ in Human Resources?

› p. 12 in digital module 1.1.A

Talking about things or jobs you did in the past.

10. I ______________________ to quit last year.
11. Two years ago I ______________________ the hospital in my current role.
12. I ______________________ him advice on how to increase his sales.

4d **Check in class. Then decide how you would say each of the sentences in your language. Do you always use the same tenses as in English?**

Tip
Use **used to + infinitive** to talk about something you once did, but no longer do: I used to work as a nurse. = I'm no longer a nurse.

4e **Complete the text with the correct forms of the verb 'work'.**

I used to *work* ______________________ as a nurse, but that was a long time ago. Now I'm a marketing manager and I ______________________ for a major automobile company. I ______________________ here for 15 years. When I started, I ______________________ in the customer services department, and then I ______________________ in sales for a few years before becoming a manager. Currently I ______________________ on a new marketing strategy.

4f **Write a similar short description of yourself and your job using different verbs (not only 'work'). Use each of the tenses, simple present, present progressive, present perfect (progressive), simple past and used to + infinitive, at least once.**

5 **In small groups: Chat about your jobs in a get-to-know-each-other situation similar to the one you heard in Audio A.06.**

› Review and AOB

Review what you have learned in this session:

1. Give three examples of new job titles that you've learned in this session.
2. Say three things about your work status, now and in the past, using the correct tenses.
3. Suggest three questions you could ask someone at an international conference about their job.

› Final feedback

What did you find most useful in this session? Tell the class. Any questions?

1 **Read the profiles below which have been provided by employees for a company website.**

TITAN
SOLUTIONS

Power tools that work as hard as you do

As an employer, TITAN has a lot to offer. Take a look behind the scenes at what our employees say about their day-to-day work and what it's like to work for us.

LIA-MARIA
PROJECT MANAGER SUSTAINABILITY

My name is Lia-Maria Gallinaro and I've been working at TITAN for six years. Since 2024 I've been responsible for a new field – sustainability. In this role, I work with my team to find out the environmental impact of our products, and I advise our business units on how to reduce their carbon footprint on a long-term basis. At the moment we're looking at the use of recycled and environmentally friendly materials in our products and packaging.

I've been in this field ever since I started my vocational training at TITAN. Now I'm working in the Electronics Service Department. I maintain and repair machines and equipment, and my job is never dull because there are always different problems to solve. I chose TITAN because it's a good employer for people like me with disabilities.

LARS
MECHATRONICS ENGINEER

SEBASTIAN
PERSONAL ASSISTANT

Hello! I'm Sebastian Harvey and I've been working as personal assistant to the managing director for the past five years. So, what do I do on a typical day? I manage her schedule, arrange travel and accommodation, coordinate meetings and events, and handle a variety of administrative tasks. Currently, I'm working on several important initiatives, including a major product launch and a new system for improving communication with other members of the management team.

2 **Look at the language used in the profiles. Make a note of examples of the following:**

a) Things people do regularly.
b) Things people are currently working on.
c) Things people have been doing for a certain length of time.

3 **Collect useful words and phrases from the profiles which you could adapt and use to describe your own job. Add the meanings in your language.**

Useful words & phrases	In my language

4 **Underline and correct the nine mistakes in the draft profile below.**

Introduction:
Felix Garcia / Sales Representative – Spain *I've worked / I've been working*

Hi! My name is Felix and I work for TITAN as a sales representative for two years. I promoting and selling our products to our customers. I giving them information and advice, and I showing them how to use TITAN power tools. Last year I have won the prize for 'Best New Titan Sales Rep'. At the moment I working on a new sales campaign for the Spanish market. I am choosing the firm TITAN because it offering great carrier opportunities.

5 **Optional extra: Write your own profile, paying special attention to the tenses you use. Present your profile to the class or display it in the next session.**

Agenda
› Introducing a new colleague
› Saying goodbye

Hello & goodbye

› Small talk

Start the session by chatting with a partner about your last weekend for a few minutes. You can, of course, move on to other topics that come up naturally. Use the following phrases in your conversation.

So, how was last weekend?

Tell me more!

› Down to business

1 **Discuss which of the information listed you would or wouldn't give in Scenario 1 and Scenario 2. Always give a reason for your decision.**

› first name | last name | age | position | marital and / or family status | nationality | current home town | current country of residence | country of origin ‹

Scenario 1:
Introducing a new colleague or customer to other business partners.

Scenario 2:
Introducing yourself to a new business partner.

A.07-08

2a **You are going to hear two conversations in which Iris Mazza introduces a new colleague to other members of staff. Read the greetings, then listen and tick (✓) the greetings you hear.**

- ☐ Good afternoon.
- ☐ How do you do?
- ☐ Hello.
- ☐ Good morning.
- ☐ Great to see you.
- ☐ Nice to meet you.
- ☐ Delighted to meet you.
- ☐ How are you?
- ☐ Hi!
- ☐ It's a pleasure to meet you.

Business Impact

Use *'How do you do?'* when you meet someone for the first time.
The answer is always to repeat back *'How do you do?'* or use *'Nice to **meet** you.'*
Use *'Nice to **see** you.'* when you meet up with someone you already know.
You can use other words instead of 'nice', of course.

2b Can you remember the details? Complete the introductions. Then listen again and check.

1. Lorenzo is ______________________ at our headquarters in Barcelona.
2. Lorenzo, this is Mr Fischer, our ______________________ .
3. Lorenzo, this is Anika Benz. She's the new ______________________ in the ______________________ .

A.07-08 2c Listen once more and complete these phrases which were used to introduce Lorenzo. Can you suggest alternatives with the same meaning?

1. ______________________ Lorenzo Valenta.
2. Please ______________________ introduce you to Lorenzo Valenta.

2d Complete these three phrases from the audio with the verbs given.

1. (meet) I've been looking forward to ______________________ you in person.
2. (see) I'll look forward to ______________________ you later on.
3. (get to know) I'm looking forward to ______________________ everyone, too.

2e In groups of three: Practise greeting and introducing each other using phrases from tasks 2a to 2d.

- Take turns to be Person A, B and C.
- You can be yourself, or invent a name and position for yourself, or choose to be one of the people on the business cards below.

Situation 1:
Person A introduces person B.
Person B is the guest.
Person C is a higher-level colleague.

Situation 2:
Person A introduces person B.
Person B is the guest.
Person C is a colleague of a similar level.

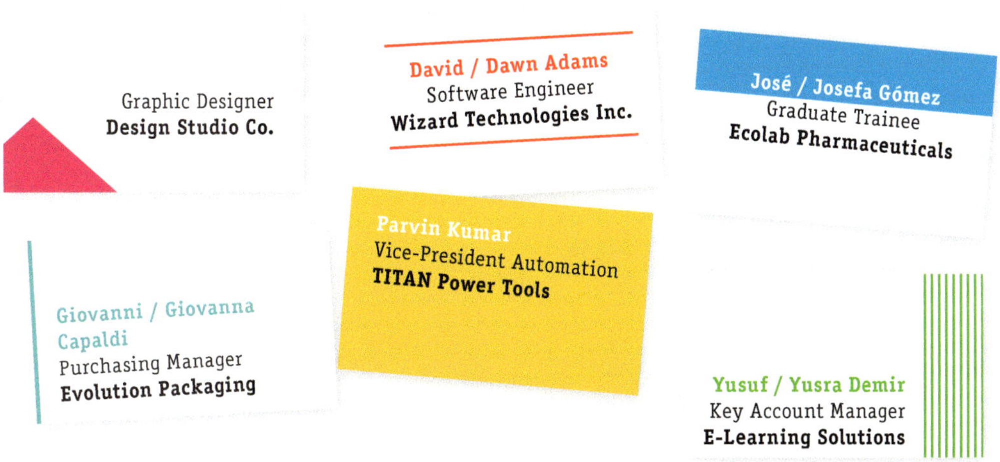

3a How many ways of saying 'goodbye' do you know in English? Collect ideas in class and create a 'Goodbye' phrase bank.

ENERGIZER

Enjoy watching this video clip.

A.3

3b Read the five short dialogues with a partner. Match each photo to one of the dialogues.

Dialogue 1

A Well, it's been great talking to you.
B Yes, we must keep in touch.
A Yes, I agree. Bye for now then.
B Bye bye.

Dialogue 2

A Catch up with you later.
B Yes, see you later! Bye!
A Bye!
B Goodbye!

Dialogue 3

A Nice meeting you, Mr / Ms … .
B And you, Ms / Mr … Goodbye.
A Goodbye. Have a safe journey.
B Thank you. Goodbye.

Dialogue 4

A I'm sorry, I must be off now or I'll miss my flight.
B Don't let me keep you. See you again soon and have a good flight.
A Thanks, goodbye!
B Bye.

Dialogue 5

A It's been a pleasure to meet you. I'm looking forward to working with you.
B Me too. Thank you for everything. I'll be in touch very soon.
A I'll look forward to hearing from you. Take care!
B Yes, goodbye.

3c Discuss these questions in class.

1. Which of the dialogues are more suitable in a formal and which in a more informal situation?
2. In each dialogue the speakers say goodbye, in one form or another, more than once. This is very common in English. What's the custom in your language?

3d Add phrases for saying goodbye from the dialogues to your phrase bank.

Tip

Keep your phrase bank at hand when making phone calls etc. in English.

3e In class. Practise short formal and informal 'Goodbye' dialogues with different partners. Use as many different goodbye phrases as possible.

4a **Look at these ways of signing off in business correspondence. Decide which you would use in a more formal context, which in a more informal context, and which you might use in either context.**

› Yours | Yours sincerely (BE) | Sincerely (AE) | Talk soon | Kind regards | See you later | Take care | Best wishes | Yours faithfully | Cheers | All the best | Bye for now ‹

Business Impact

It's likely you will come across other forms of greeting and signing off in business correspondence. If you're not sure, play safe by using a formal phrase.

4b **Add a suitable term from 4a to sign off each of the mails and messages on the right. Then compare your solutions in class. More than one solution is sometimes correct.**

4c **Add phrases from 4a to the table to create guidelines for correspondence. You can use them for future reference when you write letters, mails and messages.**

Formal correspondence		Informal correspondence	
Greeting	**Signing off**	**Greeting**	**Signing off**
Dear Sir / Madam Dear [Title + name] Dear [+ name],		Hi Hello Dear [+ name],	

From: john@doe.com
To: jane@roe.com

Dear Sir / Madam,
With reference to your job advertisement in …

Hi Lucy, Sorry, I sent you the wrong link. Oops! Here's the right one. …
10:18 ✓✓

From: john@doe.com
To: sanlav@company.com

Dear Ms Sanlav,
Please find attached …

From: john@doe.com
To: jk@doe.com; liz@doe.com; al@d

Dear all, Many thanks for attending the workshop on Friday, and …

From: john@doe.com
To: doc@bechtold.com

Dear Dr. Bechtold,
We regret to inform you that …

Hi guys, Anyone up for a drink after work today? We could meet …
9:25 ✓✓

5 **If a visitor from another country asks for advice about greetings and goodbyes in your organisation, what would you advise them? Discuss in class.**

› Review and AOB

Review what you have learned in this session:

1. Suggest a way of introducing someone in a formal and informal way.
2. Suggest three different ways of saying 'goodbye' that you can use with English-speaking colleagues.
3. Suggest two formal and two informal ways to sign off a message or email.
4. Say 'goodbye' to people in class in an appropriate way.

› Final feedback

What did you find most useful in this session? Tell the class. Any questions?

› p. 19 in digital module 1.1.A

1 **Read the following article about difficult situations that sometimes occur at work.**

Business Impact

TRICKY SITUATIONS *in the workplace*

When we're at work, situations sometimes arise which are tricky to handle or not what they seem at first sight. Here are some typical examples!

No name introductions (Keith)

When I was younger and less experienced, I used to find it really awkward when I met a colleague I knew, but couldn't remember his or her name. I quite often managed to get round the problem by avoiding using their name at all. That worked up to a point, but it got tricky when I had to introduce the person to a third person. My standard solution in those situations was to greet the third person enthusiastically, but without mentioning their name (assuming I remembered it!), by saying "Ahh, nice to see you!" or "So glad you've made it!" or "Just the person we've been waiting for!" and then go on to get both people to introduce themselves to each other: "Why don't you just introduce yourselves to each other? I'm sure you can do a better job of it than me!" It always seemed to work – even if the people concerned probably realised what my game was! Nowadays I'm just honest and admit as politely as possible that I've forgotten the name with a straightforward "I must apologise, I'm hopeless at remembering names. Would you mind telling me yours again, please?" or simply "So sorry, I know your name, but I'm having a mental block." Or if you're getting on, like me, "Sorry, your name escapes me. I'm having a senior moment." That usually attracts a smile – and so far, no-one's taken offence!

An unfriendly colleague? (Jane)

There was a colleague who got the same train to work as me, but who never used to acknowledge me on the train! I thought he just wanted his peace and quiet so I didn't bother saying hello to him either. Then one day things changed and he waved and said "Hello" to me. I was really surprised! Then, before the weekend, it happened again. "Friday at last!" he said, giving a thumbs up. There was no stopping him after that. It could be "Off home now, too?", "Had a good week?", or "Good weekend?" We get on very well now, thanks to his new contact lenses. It turns out he wasn't ignoring me after all. He was just shortsighted!

Time for dinner? (Ken)

I used to work in Germany and it took me a while before I got used to certain customs, like when my co-workers would knock on the table before leaving a meeting (a sign of appreciation in Germany, like clapping in English-speaking countries). And at midday people would greet each other by saying "Mahlzeit!" which literally means 'mealtime.' In New York if I called "Mealtime!" to my co-workers, they'd think I was nuts. "Enjoy!" or "Enjoy your meal." before digging in is the most that's required, but often we just get on with the eating! Or saying goodbye at the end of the day by calling out "Schönen Feierabend!", which I took to mean 'nice party evening.' For a long time I thought everyone was off to a party that I wasn't invited to. In the end I finally plucked up courage and asked another co-worker where the party was taking place. Everyone was very amused!

Magazine

2 **Explain each of the anecdotes in English in your own words in two or three sentences.**

› No name introduction | An unfriendly colleague? | Time for dinner? ‹

3 **How would you say these sentences from the first anecdote in your language? Write down your own version first, then compare with a version from a free online translating service and create a 'best' version.**

a) "Why don't you just introduce yourselves to each other, I'm sure you can do a better job of it than me!"

___

b) "I'm having a mental block." ___

c) "Your name escapes me." ___

d) "I'm having a senior moment." ___

4 **Read the tip about incomplete sentences in informal spoken English. Then suggest what the missing words are in these phrases from the second anecdote.**

a) "Friday at last!" ___

b) "Off home now, too?" ___

___

c) "Had a good week?" ___

___

Tip
In informal spoken English people often use incomplete sentences, in which the subject and the verb are left out.
"All right?" › "**Are you** all right?"
"Finished already?" › "**Have you** finished already?"
"Know what I mean?" › "**Do you** know what I mean?"

d) "Any plans for the weekend?" ___

5 **The third anecdote describes German customs for the situations below. What do people in your company do or say in these situations?**

a) To show appreciation at the end of a meeting or talk
b) As a greeting before going to lunch
c) To say goodbye at the end of the day

6 **Use the internet and find out what people say and do in these situations in other parts of the world that you might visit, e.g. the USA, India, Japan, China or other European countries.**

7 **Optional extra: What kind of similar tricky situation(s) have you experienced in the workplace? Make notes and prepare to tell the class about it / them in the next session.**

› Greetings and goodbyes

1 Listen. Then read the dialogues with different partners. Use your own names and positions, etc. or invent suitable alternatives for the information in *italics*.

A.09 **Dialogue 1**

A Hello, Welcome to *Sun Solutions!* I'm *Lea Swanson.*
B My name's *Raushan Öger* from *Blue Sky.* Thank you for inviting me.
A Pleased to meet you, *Mr Öger.*
B Pleased to meet you, too. It's great to be here.
A Let me introduce you to some colleagues.
B Thanks, that's very kind of you, *Ms Swanson.*

A.10 **Dialogue 2**

A Good morning, *Lea.* Nice to see you again!
B And you, too, *Gianluca.* How are you doing?
A Fine, thanks, and you?
B Not so bad, thanks!

A.11 **Dialogue 3**

A How d'you do, *Mr Öger.*
B How d'you do, *Mr Serpa.*
A It's a pleasure to meet you.
B I can only say the same in return.

A.12 **Dialogue 4**

A Hi there. I'm *Craig Watson, Head of Production* at *Sun Solutions.*
B Ah, *Craig.* Hello! It's great to finally meet you in person. I'm *Alisha Haxha.* We've talked on the phone and mailed quite a bit.
A *Alisha!* Of course! I've been looking forward to meeting you. It's good to put a face to a name at last.

A.13 **Dialogue 5**

A Good afternoon, everyone. Thank you all for coming. It's great to see so many familiar faces here today, as well as all the newcomers. Before we get down to business, may I introduce myself to anyone who doesn't know me yet? I'm *Raushan Öger, Regional Sales Manager* at *Blue Sky* and I've been in this position for …

A.14 **Dialogue 6**

A Well, it's been great talking to you. We must keep in touch.
B Yes, and I'll look forward to seeing you at the *Madrid trade show.*
A Definitely! Me, too.

A.15 **Dialogue 7**

A Goodbye, *Craig.* Have a safe journey home.
B Bye, *Alisha.* Take care. And keep me up to date on any new developments, won't you?
A Will do. And let me know if there's anything else I can do for you.
B Thanks. Bye then.
A Bye! See you again soon.

Formal follow-up message

From: oger@bluesky.com
To: serpa@company.com

Dear Mr Serpa,
It was a pleasure to get to know you and your colleagues yesterday. I look forward to hearing from you again in the near future.
Yours sincerely,
Raushan Öger / Regional Sales Manager

Informal follow-up message

From: watson@sun-solutions.com
To: alisha@haxha.com

Dear Alisha,
It was great seeing you yesterday.
Thanks for introducing me to everyone.
Let's catch up again soon.
Craig

2 In pairs. Read the dialogues again and add at least two more turns for A and B to each one.

3 How would you respond to each of these greetings?

1. How d'you do?
2. How are you?
3. Pleased to meet you.

4 Think of at least three different ways to complete these phrases.

1. It's ... to meet you.
2. Thank you for ... me.
3. I've been looking forward to ... you.
4. I ... you again in the near future.
5. Let's ... again soon.

5 Practise in threes. You are with a colleague at a conference. Follow the steps:

Step 1: You recognise the third person in your group. Greet the person formally and introduce him / her to your colleague.

Step 2: Say goodbye to each other, showing interest in future contact.

Step 3: Write a short follow-up email to the colleague you have just met, showing that you are pleased to have met and showing interest in future contact.

6 Develop new dialogues, building on phrases from the Essential phrases bank on the right.

1. Choose one phrase from each category in the phrase bank. Mark it with a highlighter.
2. Work with a partner and develop one or two new dialogues using all of your marked phrases.
3. Practise and perform your new dialogue(s) in class.

› Essential phrases

Personal greetings & responses

- Welcome to *[name of organisation]*!
  › Thank you for inviting me.
- A: How d'you do? › B: How d'you do? *(formal)*
- Good morning / afternoon / evening (everyone).
- Pleased / Nice / Delighted to meet you!
- It's a pleasure to meet you.
  › I can only say the same in return.
- It's great to be here / to finally meet you in person.
- It's good to put a face to a name at last.
- I've been looking forward to meeting you.

Introductions

- May I introduce myself (to anyone who doesn't know me yet)?
- Hello, my name's *[full name]*.
- I'm *[full name]* from *[organisation]*.
- Let me introduce you to *[name / position]* some colleagues. › Thanks, that's very kind of you.

Meeting again

- Good / Great / Nice to see you (again)!
- How are you?
- How's it going? / How are things? *(informal)*
- (I'm) Fine, / Very well, / Not so bad, thanks. And you?

Greeting a large group

- Good morning / afternoon / evening, everyone.
- Thank you all for coming.
- It's great to see so many familiar faces here today, as well as all the newcomers.
- Before we get down to business, may I introduce myself to anyone who doesn't know me yet?

Saying goodbye

- Goodbye! / Bye! / Bye for now!
- It was / It's been nice meeting you / talking to you.
- It's been a pleasure to get to know you.
- Have a safe journey / flight.
- Take care.
- See you again soon.

Showing interest in future contact

- We must keep in touch.
- Let's catch up again soon.
- I'll look / I look / I'm looking forward to seeing you.
- Keep me up to date (on ...).
- Let me know if there's anything else I can do.

Session 1

1 Which greeting would you use in which situation? Write the numbers 1 - 4 in the boxes. More than one answer may be correct.

Greetings
1. Dear Sir or Madam
2. Hi + [first name]
3. Dear Ms …
4. Ladies and Gentlemen

Situation
- a covering letter ☐ ☐ ☐ ☐
- an informal email ☐ ☐ ☐ ☐
- a formal email ☐ ☐ ☐ ☐
- a phone call ☐ ☐ ☐ ☐
- opening a meeting ☐ ☐ ☐ ☐
- welcoming visitors ☐ ☐ ☐ ☐

A.16-19 **2 Listen and tick (✓) the sentence that best describes the situation.**

a) ☐ Someone apologises to a person for making a mistake with their name.
☐ Someone tells a person they didn't hear or don't know how to say their name.
☐ Someone wants to check how to say a person's name.

b) ☐ Someone isn't sure they have heard a name properly.
☐ Someone asks a person how they prefer to be addressed.
☐ Someone tells a person how they want to be addressed.

c) ☐ Someone wants to check how to say a person's name.
☐ Someone's greeting a person face-to-face for the first time.
☐ Someone asks a person how they prefer to be addressed.

d) ☐ Someone tells a person they don't know how to pronounce their name.
☐ Someone asks a person how they prefer to be addressed.
☐ Someone apologises to a person for making a mistake with their name.

Session 2

1 Read the profile and tick the statements that are true.

a) ☐ He speaks several languages.
b) ☐ He's working for a non-profit organisation.
c) ☐ His current position is at *Media Platforms Inc.*
d) ☐ He's worked as a Data Analyst and a University Lecturer so far.
e) ☐ He began his career as a Social Media Data Analyst in 2022.
f) ☐ He did his PhD in 2016.

Dr Ron Falkner

Social Media Content Moderator at *Media Platforms Inc.*
2022-present

Message …

38-year-old multilingual enthusiast in digital content creation and community engagement, seeking new opportunities in a non-profit organisation.

Work Experience
- Social Media Data Analyst at *Paypalpable Ltd.*, 2019-2022
- Lecturer in Journalism at *Carlington University*, Ottawa, 2010-2019
- PhD (Doctorate) in Computing Language Corpora at *Carlington University*, Ottawa, 2016
- Author of a book on filtering out hate speech in social media, *You don't say!* Delta Publishing, 2020
- Volunteer at the *Ottawa Elementary School Literacy Programme* offering afternoon reading circles, since 2008

2 Correct the mistakes in the statements.

a) He's been in social media since two years.
b) He's gave university lectures for 9 years.
c) He's working as a Content Moderator since 2022.
d) He's written a book called *You don't say!* in 2020.
e) He's done his PhD at *Carlington University* in 2016.
f) He volunteers offering reading circles since 2008.

Session 3

1 Put the words in the correct order to write sentences.

a) allow Please to Henry Stark introduce you to me

____

b) she is Lorey your and team leader is This new

____

c) It pleasure is too to you a Steve meet

____

d) and am to forward meet looking to you with working you I delighted

____

e) would I Shirley Masters new marketing director you like to our meet

____

2 Choose the correct option to end a meeting appropriately.

a) It's been great …	☐ talking to you.	☐ talk to you.	☐ to talking to you.
b) We must keep …	☐ touching.	☐ touchy.	☐ in touch.
c) I'm sorry but I must be …	☐ on now.	☐ off now.	☐ out now.
d) I'm in a rush. I'll …	☐ get you later.	☐ catch up with you later.	☐ caught up later.
e) Don't let me …	☐ rushing you.	☐ catch you.	☐ keep you.
f) Have a safe journey and …	☐ take care!	☐ just take it!	☐ take off!

Business English live

1 Complete the short exchanges with suitable phrases.

A My name's Peter Marks from Intertrex. Thank you for inviting me.

B ______________________________

A How d'you do?

B ______________________________

A Bye, Lisa. Have a safe journey and keep in touch, won't you?

B ______________________________

2 How would you say the following?

I'd like you to stay in contact with me.

____

I'd like to know about any news of yours in the future.

____

I've known you from mails and phone calls and I'm happy to meet you face-to-face now.

____

NAMING THE BABY

How did you get your name? Were you named after a saint, a king or queen or even a celebrity? Does your name run in the family or was it just a fashionable name at the time? Your parents' choices may have been limited. The name Tom is banned in Portugal, for example, and in Germany, gender-neutral names and surnames used as first names are forbidden. Elon Musk got away with calling his son X Æ A-Xii, who goes by the name 'X', yet in the US it is against the law to name a child 'Santa Claus' or 'Nutella'. In the UK, where almost anything goes, naming your baby 'Cyanide' is a no-no.

Similar factors affect the choice of a company name. In the past, founders typically named their companies after themselves (Ford, McDonald's, Prada) but the trend today is to be more creative. Some founders play with their names. Adolph Dassler combined his nick-name 'Adi' with the first three letters of his surname to create 'Adidas'. The singers in the Swedish band ABBA used the first letters of their names. T.E. Stockwell and J. Cohen merged to become TESCO. The name 'Haribo' comes from the company's founder and his hometown in Germany: Hans Riegel, Bonn. If the name of the founder is not used, there are other ways to give a company personality, such as deliberately mispelling the name ('Google' from the number googol), or mixing languages (Häägen-Daz).

Inventing a completely new name can be a minefield, especially for companies with global ambitions. Often an English translation of the name is chosen, but even that can be tricky. The Japanese company Tokyo Tsushin Kogyo decided against 'Tokyo Telecommunications Engineering Company' (too long) and it couldn't be shortened to 'TKK' (already used by another Japanese company). Instead, the name Sony was chosen, from the Latin 'sonus' (sound) and the American expression 'sonny boy'. For Akio Morita, head of Sony America, this evoked "the youthful energy and irreverence he wanted at the heart of the company". Also, the name would be pronounceable in many languages.

Some names are so popular, they become verbs. The original name for Google was 'BackRub', a fun fact you can google for yourselves. So, before you choose a name for your business, ask yourself if it is meaningful, legal, and easy to spell and say – even as a verb.

Share

1 **Before you read: What's your organisation called? Do you know where the name comes from?**

2 **Find phrases in the article for explaining the origin of names, e.g., 'named after …', 'It comes from …'.**

3 **Complete the following questions with the correct form (adjective, verb, noun) of the word in brackets. Be careful with past forms.**

1. (choice) Do you know who ______________________ the name of your organisation?
2. (origin) Can you explain how the name ______________________ ?
3. (combine) Is it a ______________________ of different elements?
4. (long) What do you think about the ______________________ of the name?
5. (short) Is it sometimes ______________________ ?
6. (strong) Does it have positive connotations, e.g. of health or ______________________ ?
7. (memory) Is the name unique, catchy and ______________________ ?
8. (pronunciation) Is it easy to ______________________ ?

4 **In class, answer the questions in task 3 about your own organisation, or one you know well.**

5 **Quiz time! Match the company to the origin of its name.**

› 7-Eleven | DHL | Esso | KFC | Lego | Palmolive | Samsonite | Starbucks | Volvo | Vodafone ‹

1. ____________ The two oils used in soap manufacture
2. ____________ Voice, Data, Telefone
3. ____________ Latin for 'I roll', because the parent company originally produced ball bearings
4. ____________ Named after its founders, Adrian Dalsey, Larry Hillblom, and Robert Lynn
5. ____________ Danish for 'Play well'
6. ____________ Shortened to avoid the unhealthy connotations of the word 'fried'
7. ____________ A character in the Herman Melville novel, *Moby-Dick*
8. ____________ A biblical character known for his strength
9. ____________ How the initials S.O. are pronounced in Standard Oil of New Jersey
10. ____________ Chosen to reflect the extended opening hours, 7:00 am to 11:00 pm

6 **Do you know any fun facts about company names? Give examples.**
Suggest a further tip for choosing a company name.

 › p. 27 in digital module 1.1.A

SAY GOODBYE TO MR AND MRS

You may think of banks as conservative, but even they are trying to move with the times. Now, it seems that the titles Mr, Mrs, Ms and the gender-neutral Mx, are no longer enough. One leading bank has introduced ten new titles for people to choose from on official forms. These include 'Ind' for individual, 'Mre' for mystery, 'Pr' for person, 'Msr' a mix of miss / sir and 'Misc' for miscellaneous. The change allows people who do not identify with a particular gender, or who prefer not to be identified by gender, to choose a title that suits them.

While there are good arguments for gender-neutral pronouns, these new titles may do more harm than good. Rather than liberating us, they do the opposite. They force us to be very specific about how we define ourselves, even when it is irrelevant. Nobody wants to be pigeonholed. So, why not get rid of these titles altogether? Some may be useful in professional contexts, such as 'Dr' and 'Professor', but what about the others?

Even if it were possible to say goodbye to Mr and Mrs, it is likely that new ways of showing respect would emerge over time. Research has shown that all languages, and therefore all people, use politeness strategies. By using Mr (which comes from Master) and Mrs (which comes from Mistress and includes Miss and Ms), we create a respectful distance between ourselves and the person we are addressing. Different languages have their own ways of achieving this, and titles don't always come before names. Gandhi was addressed by his followers as Gandhi-ji. The suffix 'ji' indicates respect, and doesn't refer to gender. Of course, one can show respect without using titles. Many Quakers avoid titles altogether for the sake of simplicity and equality. Schoolchildren call their teachers by their first (or given) name, and this is not seen as a sign of disrespect. You might feel that being on a first-name basis with your bank manager is a step too far. So, what about using full names without titles? Or just using surnames? If we really want to show respect, there's always the option of using the gender-neutral multipurpose suffix 'ji'. Or we could invent something similar. Maybe the simplest option is to follow what others do. If your bank manager calls you 'Sir', call him 'Sir' (or 'Madam'). When in Rome, do as the Romans.

The bank claims it has redesigned its online form to be more inclusive. If this is the case, are ten options enough? The drop-down menu on the website of Fortnum & Mason, a London department store, has 56 options, and it doesn't even have 'Ind' and 'Mr'. But is the whole issue really just about inclusivity? Maybe there's another reason why companies ask for our titles. It could be the marketing team's way of putting us into demographic categories. So, if you choose the option 'HRH' (His / Her Royal Highness) when you buy a luxury food hamper, they already know a lot about you.

Share

1 **Before you read: When filling in a form, which options do you expect to find under the heading 'Title'? Which options do you think should be included (or deleted)?**

2 **While reading: Make a list of the titles that are mentioned in the article and what each one stands for. (Add the information yourself if necessary.)**

Mr - to address a man, ______

______

3 **Which of the titles mentioned do you use or have you used? What are the equivalent titles in your own language?**

4 **Discuss these questions in class.**

1. What kind of titles do you think the writer of the article is referring to in the question: *'Why not get rid of these titles altogether?'* What's your opinion on using or getting rid of titles?
2. How did you refer to your teachers when you were at school? How do you address people, such as your bank manager, doctor, superiors at work, etc.?
3. Has the way you address people changed? Would you like to make any changes? How, and why?
4. Would you ever insist that someone uses your title? Why or why not?

5 **Read the definitions of 'pigeonhole'. Then discuss the questions below.**

pi•geon•hole /ˈpɪdʒən.həʊl/

pigeonhole (noun):	one of a set of small open boxes fixed to a wall, where letters and messages may be left for individuals
to pigeonhole (verb):	to unfairly consider a person as belonging to a particular type or group

1. Do you have a pigeonhole at work? What is it used for?
2. In your opinion, does having a wider range of titles to choose from lead to people being 'pigeonholed'? How useful is a wide range of titles for marketing purposes?

6 **Discussion: Work in pairs or two groups, A and B, and discuss the statement: 'The more titles people have to choose from the better.'**

A You are in favour of having a wide range of titles to choose from.
B You are against having a wide range of titles to choose from.

1. Note down arguments to support 'your' point of view. These can include ideas from the article and / or your own ideas.

______

______

______

2. Have a discussion in which each side puts forward 'their' point of view using their arguments.

 › p. 29 in digital module 1.1.A

Meeting *request!*

Agenda
- › Arranging a meeting
- › Confirming attendance
- › Turning down a request

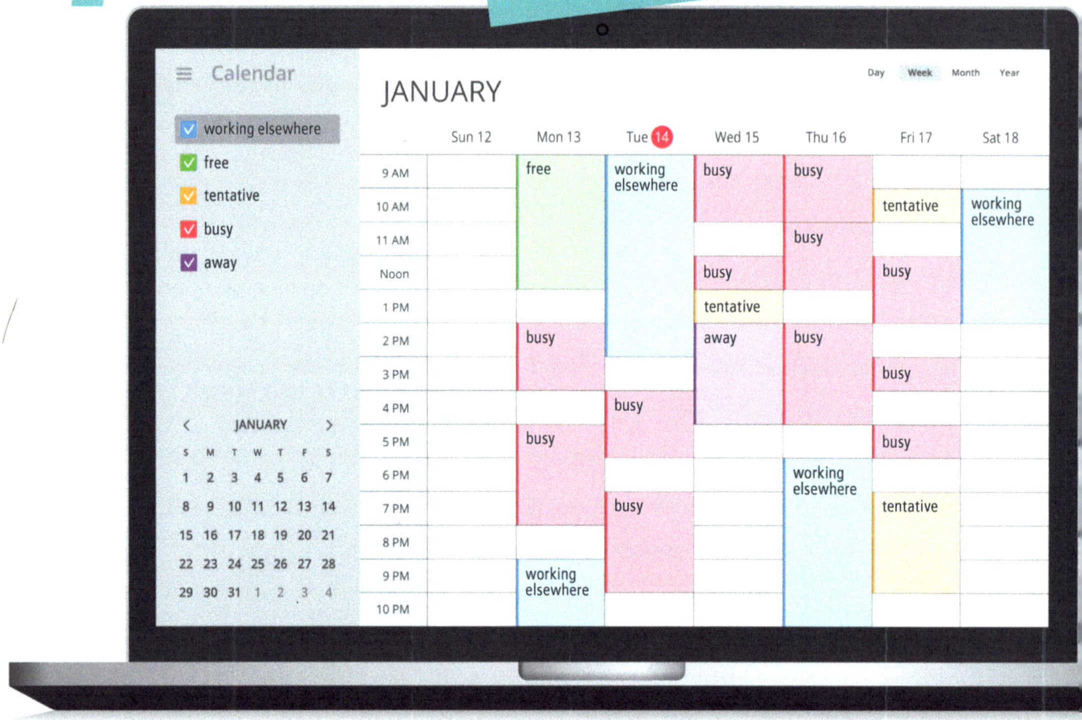

› Small talk

Start the session by chatting with a partner about your plans for the weekend for a few minutes. Your conversation can, of course, move on to other topics that come up naturally. Use the following phrases in your conversation.

I'm really looking forward to …

I can't wait to …

Tip
A quick chat at the beginning of every English class is a great opportunity to practise and improve your small talk skills.

› Down to business

1 Discuss your work schedules in class. Use these questions as a starting point.

1. How similar is the calendar above to your own?
2. How do you usually arrange meetings at work and / or at home?
3. What's your schedule for this week in terms of meetings and appointments?

B.01

2a Listen to a phone call in which two colleagues arrange a meeting. Note down details about the proposed meeting.

2b Compare your notes with a partner to check you have got all the correct information.

2c In the following phrases, an alternative option is provided. Which option was used in the audio?

1. I just wondered whether you're **free / available** to join a catch-up meeting on Wednesday.
2. Let me just check my **diary / calendar.**
3. I'm afraid I can't **make it on / do** Wednesday afternoon.
4. How about the morning **instead / as an alternative?**
5. **I'm also free / I can also make it** on Thursday from three pm.
6. Thursday from three would **be fine / work well** for me.
7. Are you thinking online or **in person / face-to-face?**
8. I'd definitely **rather / prefer** in person – unless that's a problem for you?
9. Is it **just us two / the two of us ?** Or who else will be attending?

Tip

Start a 'Meetings' phrase bank with the phrases in 2c, so you have them at hand when organising your own meetings in English. Add to your phrase bank throughout the session.

2d Both options above are correct. Which option would you feel most comfortable using? Compare with a partner.

2e In pairs. Practise arranging a meeting in similar calls to the call in the audio.

1. Note down the following things first:
   - possible dates for the meeting
   - is the meeting online or in person?
   - how long you expect the meeting to be
   - how many people you want to invite (names and positions)
   - the topic that you want to discuss

2. Take it in turns to arrange a meeting using as many phrases from task 2c as possible.

› p. 5 in digital module 1.1.B

3a Compare the formal and informal written meeting requests below. Identify the different ways in which similar things are expressed in both emails.

Formal meeting request

From: mia@rogers.com
To: office@company.com

Dear Tom, Chris and Helen,

I hope you are well. I am writing to confirm the date of our next team meeting, which is scheduled for Thursday at 3 pm.
As soon as a meeting room has been booked, I'll let you know.
The aim of the meeting is to discuss the new automated chat system we are thinking of introducing.
Attached you will find the agenda.
Would you please read this and let me know if you have any questions?
I would appreciate it if you would keep an hour free for the meeting at this stage.
If you are unable to attend, please let me know as soon as possible.
I look forward to seeing you all there.

Kind regards,
Mia Rogers

Informal meeting request

From: mia@rogers.com
To: office@company.com

Hi everyone,

How are things? I'm just confirming our next team meeting on Thursday at 3.
We'll be discussing the new automated chat system we might set up. We'll probably need about an hour.
I've attached the agenda for you to take a look at. Get back to me if you have any questions.
Let me know if you can't make it.
Looking forward to seeing you!

Cheers,
Mia

PS I'll get in touch as soon as I know which room we're in.

3b Add phrases and / or key words from the emails to the table below.

	Formal meeting request	Informal meeting request
Addressing participants	*Dear …,*	*Hi everyone,*
Suggesting dates and times		
Referring to content of meeting		
Referring to attachments		
Requesting attention		
Requesting return message		
Signing off		

3c Write a formal and an informal meeting request for the meeting you planned by phone in task 2e, or for an upcoming meeting you are attending or planning.

- Refer to the emails in 3a and the table in 3b for assistance.
- Write a formal meeting request for the meeting first.
- Rewrite your formal meeting request as an informal request.

Tip
Add useful phrases from the table to your 'Meetings' phrase bank.

› p. 6 in digital module 1.1.B

ENERGIZER

Enjoy watching this video clip.

▶ B.1

4a Read the responses to the meeting request below.

Which response A, B or C is:

1. confirming attendance? ☐
2. rejecting the invitation? ☐
3. suggesting an alternative? ☐

From: mia@rogers.com
To: office@company.com

Dear Tom, Chris and Helen,
I hope you are well. I am writing to confirm the date of our next team meeting, which is scheduled for Thursday at 3 pm. As soon as a meeting room has been booked, I'll let you know. The aim of the meeting is to discuss the new automated chat system

A

From: helen@company.com
To: mia@rogers.com

Dear Mia,
Please accept my apologies, but unfortunately, I will not be able to attend the meeting on Thursday. I have a meeting planned with a client in Manchester on that day.
Best wishes,
Helen

B

From: tom@company.com
To: mia@rogers.com

Hi Mia,
I've managed to move something in my calendar, so I'll be able to attend the meeting. Can I give you a quick call about the agenda?
Best,
Tom

C

From: chris@company.com
To: mia@rogers.com

Dear Mia,
I wouldn't be able to attend the meeting on Thursday. But I have a lot of flexibility the following week. Would it be possible to postpone the meeting and find an alternative date?
Regards,
Chris

4b Request a meeting & respond to a request.

1. 'Send' your formal and informal meeting requests from task 3c to two different members of your class (on paper, via chat, via email …).
2. Respond to the meeting requests you receive appropriately. You can confirm, reject and / or suggest an alternative date.

› Review and AOB

Review what you have learned in this session:

1. Suggest three phrases for arranging a meeting on the phone.
2. Suggest examples of differences in language used in formal and informal meeting requests.
3. Suggest one way to confirm attendance, to excuse yourself and to suggest an alternative day or time for a meeting.

› Final feedback

What did you find most useful in this session? Tell the class. Any questions?

1 Finding a meeting time that suits everyone isn't always easy. The following email thread is a typical example.

Tip

Reading an email thread from bottom to top rather than top to bottom, often helps make sense of it.

From: David; **Sent:** 10 March 11:09; **To:** Belle, Paula, Ana; **Subject:** Re: Re: Re: Re: Re: Re: Team meeting

Ok, thanks everyone. I'll get back to you all with the final date and time later today.
David

From: Belle; **Sent:** 10 March 11:03; **To:** David, Paula, Ana; **Subject:** Re: Re: Re: Re: Re: Team meeting

Hi
Monday would be best for me. Wednesday is out for me. I might be able to do Thursday if we start later. I could be there anytime after 3 if that would work for everyone?
Belle

From: Paula; **Sent:** 10 March 10:50; **To:** David, Belle, Ana; **Subject:** Re: Re: Re: Re: Team meeting

An all-day meeting? Poor you!
I could maybe do Wednesday or Thursday, but from 5 pm after the event.
How does Wednesday or Thursday at 5 pm suit everyone? Would that work instead?
Paula

From: David; **Sent:** 10 March 10:42; **To:** Belle, Paula, Ana; **Subject:** Re: Re: Re: Team meeting

Sorry, Paula, but Tuesday isn't possible for me – I'm meeting a client then and we have an all-day meeting that I can't change.
David

From: Paula; **Sent:** 10 March 10:37; **To:** David, Belle, Ana; **Subject:** Re: Re: Team meeting

Hello everyone,
Sorry, but I'm at an event Wednesday to Friday. How about Tuesday instead?
Monday would also be fine for me.
Paula

From: Ana; **Sent:** 10 March 10:25; **To:** David, Belle, Paula; **Subject:** Re: Team meeting

Hi all,
Thanks for your mail, David. Wednesday morning works for me. And Thursday afternoon is OK as well, anytime from 3 onwards. (Then my partner's home and can take care of the kids.)
Monday's my day off, so I'm out of the office then, I'm afraid.
Ana

From: David; **Sent:** 10 March 10:15; **To:** Belle, Paula, Ana; **Subject:** Team meeting

Hi everyone,
It's probably not going to be possible to meet face-to-face next week as we all have a lot on, so I suggest a video call. I can do Monday 10th or Wednesday 12th from 9:30 or Thursday 14th from 1 pm. Could you all reply asap and let me know which of these times suit you, please?
Thanks
David

2 **Work out when the best time for the meeting would be. Then complete the following email from David to the participants confirming the final meeting time.**

From: David, **Sent:** 10 March 14:16
To: Belle, Paula, Ana
Subject: Re:Re:Re:Re:Re:Re:Re: Team meeting

Hi everyone,

Here's confirmation of our meeting. It'll be on ______________, ______________ starting at ______________, so that hopefully everyone can attend.

Best, David

3 **Focus on words & phrases: Find the words and phrases used to say the following.**

a) David: to say that he'll send a message to everyone

b) Belle: to say that a time or date is impossible

c) David / Paula: to describe a meeting that goes on for a whole day

d) Paula: to say 'as an alternative'

e) Ana: to say that she's not working on a particular day

f) David: to say everyone is very busy

4 **Add phrases from the email thread to the table. Consider adding useful phrases from the table to your 'Meetings' phrase bank.**

Responding to meeting requests

Confirming attendance	Rejecting an invitation	Suggesting alternative dates
Wednesday works for me.	*Sorry, but …*	*How about … instead?*

Agenda
- Formal agendas
- Handling a meeting successfully

Meetings & *agendas*

"Surely somebody must know why we're here?"

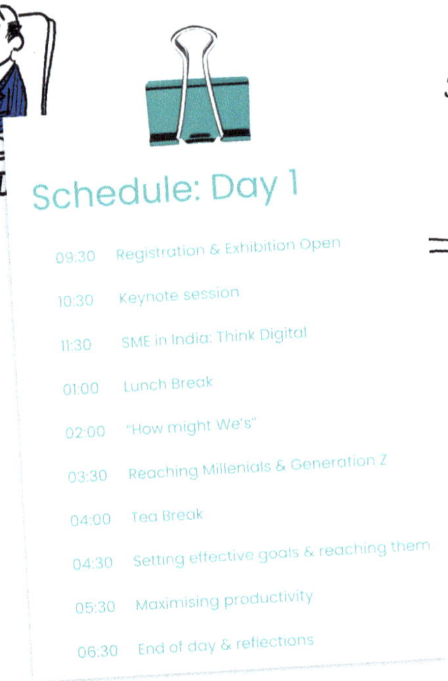
Schedule: Day 1

09:30	Registration & Exhibition Open
10:30	Keynote session
11:30	SME in India: Think Digital
01:00	Lunch Break
02:00	"How might We's"
03:30	Reaching Millenials & Generation Z
04:00	Tea Break
04:30	Setting effective goals & reaching them
05:30	Maximising productivity
06:30	End of day & reflections

› Small talk

Start the session by chatting with a partner for a few minutes about the last time you went on an outing with colleagues or friends. Your conversation can, of course, move on to other topics that come up naturally. Use the phrases on the right in your conversation.

We had a … time!

You're kidding, aren't you?

› Down to business

1 **Look at the cartoons and discuss the following questions in class.**

1. What point is each cartoon making about meetings?
2. Which cartoon is most typical of meetings in general and of meetings you attend?
3. How well structured are meetings that you attend in terms of agendas and timekeeping?

 › p. 10 in digital module 1.1.B

2a **Below is the agenda for the upcoming meeting (from Session 1). How similar or different is this agenda to agendas for your meetings?**

2b **Study the agenda and answer the questions.**

1. Which headings on the agenda tell you …

a) who is heading the meeting?

____

b) who is expected to come to the meeting?

____

c) when the meeting will take place?

____

d) where the meeting will take place?

____

2. What do these abbreviations stand for?

a) AOB ______________________

b) TS, etc. ______________________

____

c) TBC ______________________

Customer Service
Team Meeting 5

Host: Mia Palmer
Attendees: Tom Smith, Chris Johnson, Helen Samuels
Date: 12/05
Time: 14:00
Venue: Meeting Room 2

Agenda

1	Approval of minutes of last team meeting
2	Update on action points from previous meeting (All)
3	Update on research (TS)
4	Presentation of beta version of chatbot (CJ)
5	Overview of focus group results (HS)
6	AOB

Date of the next meeting
The next meeting date has not yet been confirmed. (TBC)

Action Points

3a **On an agenda, items are written as concisely as possible, often by starting with a noun and omitting the articles *(the, a* or *an).* Find examples in the agenda. Which words are missing?**

Example: Approval of minutes of last team meeting › Approval of the minutes of the last team meeting

3b **Read the email. Use the information to create an agenda. Compare your agendas in class.**

3c **Online AI* tools can be used to create agendas too. Try it out.**

1. Enter the information from the email into the AI tool of your choice.
2. Compare the result with your own agenda.
3. Come up with a 'best' solution in class.
4. Compare your own versions.

From: james@gilmore.com
To: office@company.com

Hi there,
Could you draw up the agenda for our meeting on 16th July for me, please? We're starting at 9:30. Could you invite Helen Abrey, Javier Turay, and Nick Manos, please? Once we've approved the minutes of the last meeting, we'll need to have an update on the action points from the last meeting. Helen will have to demonstrate the latest version of the app. Javier will need to give a presentation on market research. And Nick will have to update us on the marketing plan for the launch. By the way, I haven't booked a meeting room yet. I'll let everyone know when it's booked.
Thanks for your help.
James Gilmore

* AI = Artificial Intelligence

B.02 **4a** **You are going to hear three extracts from a meeting. Read the comprehension questions for part 1. Then listen and note down the answers.**

1. When does the meeting start and when will it end?

____

2. Why was Chris late? ______________________________
3. Which 'rules' for the meeting does Mia suggest in order to get through the agenda quickly?

____

4b **Listen again. This time focus on what Mia says and note down the phrases.**

What does Mia say …

1. to start the meeting once everyone is there? ______________________________

____

2. to check that everyone has the agenda? ______________________________
3. to tell people to turn off their microphones? ______________________________
4. to point out that she wants the meeting to end on time? ______________________________
5. to tell the attendees not to talk for too long? ______________________________

B.03 **5a** **Read the comprehension questions for part 2. Then listen and note down the answers.**

1. Why does Mia interrupt Chris? ______________________________
2. What does Chris offer to do? ______________________________

5b **Now focus on what Mia says and note down the phrases used. Listen again, if necessary.**

What does Mia say …

1. to interrupt Chris? ______________________________
2. to continue with the meeting? ______________________________

B.04 **6a Read the comprehension questions for part 3. Then listen and note down the answers.**

1. What does Helen need to arrange? ______
2. How long will it take? ______

6b Now focus on the language in part 3 and note down the phrases Mia uses. Listen again, if necessary.

What does Mia say …

1. when she can't hear Helen? ______
2. that she wants to be kept up to date? ______
3. to end the meeting? ______

7a Role play. In small groups, imagine a meeting you might take part in. Write a dialogue for the meeting using as many phrases from this session as possible. Your meeting must include the following three elements:

1 The beginning of the meeting
2 Moving from one agenda item to another
3 Ending the meeting

______
______
______
______
______
______
______

ENERGIZER

Enjoy watching this video clip.

B.2

Tip

You can use online AI tools to create dialogues in English. Why not give it a try?

7b Practise, then perform your meeting to the class.

Review and AOB

Review what you have learned in this session:

1. Name the main components you'd expect to find in an agenda.
2. Suggest two or three different phrases for starting a meeting.
3. Suggest two or three different phrases for ending a meeting.

Final feedback

What did you find most useful in this session? Tell the class. Any questions?

1 **Before you read: Note down your personal three top tips for successful meetings.**

a) ____________________

b) ____________________

c) ____________________

2 **Now read the article and answer the questions.**

a) Which of your tips are mentioned?
b) Focus on the first part of article (Tips 1 to 6). Which three tips do you think are most useful?
c) Which of the three tips given for remote meetings do you consider most valuable?
d) Write one more tip for both parts of the article and give your tips a suitable heading.

3 **Focus on language: Useful phrases (verb + noun or collocation)**
Find the phrases in the text which mean the following:

a) to set times for each point › *to allocate timeframes*

b) to allow enough time or space for something › ____________________

c) to present a schedule › ____________________

d) to make sure the meeting flows smoothly › ____________________

e) to give people specific tasks › ____________________

f) to end on time › ____________________

g) to review things that have been decided › ____________________

h) to define what will happen next › ____________________

i) to focus fully on something › ____________________

j) to build a good relationship with others › ____________________

4 **Use verbal phrases from task 3 to complete this post-meeting message.**

Hi there! What a disastrous meeting! Mark forgot ____________________ (1) the agenda at the beginning, and he didn't ____________________ (2), so no one took minutes. He hadn't ____________________ (3) for the items either and he let everyone talk for ages, so we didn't ____________________ (4) – as usual! It was Julia's turn to moderate, so she was supposed to be ____________________ (5) but actually she was ____________________ (6) her mails, I think. All in all, it was a total waste of time! Lucky for you, you weren't there! 10:18 ✓✓

Top tips for meetings

Successful meetings, whether remote or in person involve more than just sending out a meeting request. With that in mind, here are some tips for making sure your meetings are always a success.

1 Keep it structured.

Create an agenda in advance of the meeting with input from attendees, if necessary. Allocate timeframes for each section and leave room for Q&A's or a discussion at the end. Share the agenda before the session and at the start of the meeting.

What to say at the meeting: "I'm just going to run through the agenda. First we'll be …, next we'll … . We'll go on to … There'll be time for questions at the end of the meeting / each item."

2 Plan ice breakers.

Ice breakers are a great way to make people feel comfortable in a meeting environment, especially if they don't know each other. Do a round of introductions and, as an ice breaker, ask everyone to share something interesting about themselves.

What to say: "I'd like to invite everyone to briefly introduce themselves. As well as telling us your name and position / organisation, I'd like to ask you to share an interesting fact about yourself with us. I'll begin …"

3 Appoint a lead or moderator.

Choose someone on your team to steer the meeting. They will need to make sure everyone sticks to the allocated time frame.

What to say:
Host: "[Name], would you please act as moderator for this meeting?"
Moderator: "Does anyone have any further points to add?"

4 Assign roles.

It's a good idea to assign roles before the meeting starts, especially who will be taking notes / minutes. Assigning these details beforehand will ensure a smoother meeting.

What to say: "[Name], would you please take notes / the minutes today?"

5 Set & stick to your time limits.

Take time limits seriously and respect a hard stop time.

What to say: "I'm afraid I'll have to stop you there, …" "We need to finish promptly [at time], so I'm afraid that's all we have time for today."

6 Recap decisions and to-dos at the end of meeting.

Ensure that your meeting isn't a waste of time by recapping decisions and clearly establishing the next steps at the end.

What to say: "Just to recap: The following decisions have been made today: … " "These are the action points: …"

And here are our three top tips for remote meetings:

1 Don't multitask! Make sure you give your undivided attention to the meeting. It's common courtesy.
2 Mute when you're not talking. Nobody wants to hear your cat meowing in the background. Unmuted people are distracting and can derail a remote meeting.
3 Turn your camera on. A face-to-face conversation is critical in establishing rapport and good teamwork, so it is important to have a camera on.

Agenda
› Writing minutes
› Using the passive voice

Minutes & more

"Just reading the minutes back will be sufficient."

"Mrs. Carstairs will read her blog of the last meeting."

› Small talk

Start the session by chatting with a partner for a few minutes about the last time you met up with colleagues socially, for example, for lunch or after work. Your conversation can, of course, move on to other topics that come up naturally. Use the following phrases in your conversation.

We ended up talking about …

Tell me / us more!

› Down to business

1 Discuss the following questions in class.

1. How important is it to have minutes of meetings in your opinion?
2. When minutes are kept, who usually writes them in meetings that you attend?
3. What should and / or shouldn't be included in the minutes of a meeting in your opinion?

2a After the meeting (in Session 2) the following minutes were sent out to all involved. Read the minutes and highlight the verbs. What verb structure is the most common? Why do you think this form is used?

2b What other features can you identify that you would expect to find in minutes in general?

Tip

The passive voice
- is formed with the appropriate form of the verb 'be' + past participle of the 'main' verb.
- is often used in formal texts and / or when you don't know, or don't want to say, who performed an action.

Team Meeting 5
Minutes

Date:	12/05, 14:00-15:45
Present:	TS, CJ, HS, MP
Absent:	None
Place:	Meeting Room 2

1 Approval of minutes of meeting on 10/04
- A motion to approve the minutes of the previous meeting was made by MP and was seconded by TS.

2 Update on action points
- Good progress is being made on all action points.
- Chatbot development is taking longer than expected.

3 Update on research
- Customer research is still being analysed.
- Further customer research needs to be carried out asap.
- Futher research to be conducted by TS.

4 Presentation of Beta version of chatbot
- Various options were discussed (see appendix: Chatbot update)
- Updated version will be supplied by CJ by the end of the month.
- New focus group to be formed to trial the new system.

5 Overview of focus group results
- Feedback from focus group was generally positive.
- However, chatbot option was rejected by about 10% of respondents who wanted to speak to an actual person.

6 AOB / Matters Arising
- Latest sales customer response times were not available from all regions. ML to contact customer service managers for an update.
- A new app developer in China is currently being trialled.
- Team meeting next week is cancelled because of trade fair.

Next meeting
In two weeks. Time & place tbc (MP)

3a Underline phrases using the passive voice in the minutes.

3b Find an example of each of these passive tense forms in the minutes. Add one example to each tense form.

Simple present *Team meeting next week is cancelled because of trade fair.*

Present progressive ______________________

____

Simple past ______________________

____

Future ______________________

Passive infinitive ______________________

Modal + passive ______________________

4 You are going to listen to four extracts from the next team meeting. Listen to each audio and complete the information in the minutes, using passive forms whenever possible.

Team Meeting 6
Minutes

Date: 26/05, 13:00-14:15
Present: TS, CJ, HS, MP
Absent: None

B.05

1 Approval of minutes of meeting on 12/05

1. The minutes from the last meeting ______________________ (1) by MP and ______________________ (2) by TS.

B.06

2 Update on action points

2. A feature telling people they are talking to a chatbot ______________________ (3).
3. The feature to switch to a person ______________________ (4) in the first few weeks. Danger: people might not choose the chatbot.
4. The switch feature ______________________ (5) in the final version.

B.07

3 Latest chatbot update

5. The latest chatbot version ______________________ (6) later today.
6. The chatbot personality ______________________ (7) to make it more friendly.
7. The new personality ______________________ (8) in the latest version this afternoon.

B.08

4 AOB / Matters Arising

8. All but one holiday request ______________________ (9).
9. At the FDL conference HS and TS ______________________ (10) the team.
10. Anyone else who wants to go should contact HS asap, so that rooms ______________________ (11).

Next meeting
In two weeks. Time & place tbc (MP)

ENERGIZER
Enjoy watching this video clip.
B.3

5a You are going to listen to a podcast discussing online and face-to-face meetings. Before you listen: Which kind of meetings do people in your class prefer, online or face-to-face? Do a quick show of hands in class to find out.

Business Impact

A show of hands can be a good way to quickly confirm motions and decisions, or to find out the majority opinion or choice in a meeting.

B.09 **5b** Listen and add the arguments for and against online meetings.

Online meetings: For	Online meetings: Against

B.10 **5c** Now listen and add the arguments for and against face-to-face meetings.

Face-to-face meetings: For	Face-to-face meetings: Against

5d In pairs. Consider more arguments for and against both kinds of meetings and add one more idea to each heading.

5e Group discussion: Which meetings are better: online or face-to-face? Think about the organisation you work for and its meeting and travelling policies. Follow the steps:

1. Form two groups. Group A is in favour of online meetings. B is in favour of face-to-face meetings.
2. Collect arguments in favour of your group's position. Refer back to your answers to tasks 5b and 5c.
3. Consider arguments the other group might come up with. Find arguments to counter these.
4. Have a discussion with the other group. Make sure everyone has the chance to speak.
5. Vote with a show of hands at the end of the discussion. Is the result still the same as in task 5a?

› Review and AOB

Review what you have learned in this session:

1. Give examples of the headings you'd expect to find in all meeting minutes.
2. Which tense is most frequently used when writing minutes? Give an example showing its use.
3. Give one advantage and one disadvantage of online and face-to-face meetings.

› Final feedback

What did you find most useful in this session? Tell the class. Any questions?

› p. 19 in digital module 1.1.B

1 Read the following article about the personality types you find at meetings.

Business Impact

WHO'S WHO *at meetings*

We've all been there: we enter a meeting room (virtually or for real) and, just by looking at the faces around the table, we immediately know how the meeting will go.

Over there on the left, with a broad smile on his face, is our friend, **Domi Nant.** He's so confident, he can dominate any meeting, even if he's not the host. He certainly doesn't need any encouragement to participate. Domi will express his opinion to anyone willing to listen and can be so focused on what he is saying that he forgets to listen to others.

On the other side of the table there's **Lotta Say.** She's extrovert and very enthusiastic, she thinks out loud and always has a lot to say. She's guaranteed to be the cause of an agenda not being followed and recording minutes of her contributions is almost impossible!

Next to Domi we have **Stan Alytical.** He's very shy and introverted. Of all the people in the room, you can be sure that Stan has analysed the minutes of the last meeting and has checked out all the points on the agenda. Unfortunately, he hardly ever says anything at meetings. When he speaks, he rarely looks people in the eye, but his comments are generally very perceptive. After the meeting you sadly often can't remember if he was there at all.

Next there's the ever-cheerful **Amy Able.** She doesn't like conflict of any kind and is always very happy to go along with the majority opinion. She hates any kind of pressure, especially the pressure when decisions need to be made by her.

And finally, next to Lotta we have **Ian Terrupter:** the one who won't let others finish what they are saying. He constantly interrupts everyone mid-sentence, and always has questions that need to be answered immediately. He makes timekeeping and sticking to an agenda virtually impossible for the chairperson and writing minutes is a nightmare thanks to his interruptions.

Understanding the personality types of your meeting participants can help you manage a meeting far more effectively. To handle **Domi Nant,** you need to make sure he knows his opinions and viewpoints have been heard. By prompting others to speak you can ensure Domi is not controlling everything that is being said!

Be prepared to gently remind **Lotta Say** to stay on track and allow others who have not spoken the opportunity to participate. You could consider setting a time limit for individual's contributions. When Lotta's time is up, she has to remain silent.

To get more out of **Stan Alytical,** make sure all documents are shared before the meeting, giving him time to think through the issues. Patience is needed when waiting for Stan to contribute but it can be worth the wait.

Don't let **Amy Able** go along with the majority by asking her for her opinion first. She won't be able to just agree with everyone then. As she hates the pressure when decisions need to be made by her, don't put her on the spot in the meeting, instead, let her know what decisions will need to be taken by her beforehand. Finally, **Ian Terrupter** needs a firm hand! Don't let him interrupt! Warn him that everyone must be allowed to finish what they are saying.

Magazine

2 **Write one sentence summarising each of the personalities described in the article.**

a) Domi Nant: ______________________________

b) Lotta Say: ______________________________

c) Stan Alytical: ______________________________

d) Amy Able: ______________________________

e) Ian Terrupter: ______________________________

3 **Focus on words: Which adjectives are used in the article to describe each personality type? Add one more adjective that would suit each personality.**

a) Domi: ______________________________

b) Lotta: ______________________________

c) Stan: ______________________________

d) Amy: ______________________________

e) Ian: ______________________________

4 **An online thesaurus can help you find new ways to express things. Look up the words in bold in an online thesaurus. (The paragraph numbers are in brackets.) Which options do you find? Which is the most appropriate in the context of the article?**

Tip
Enter 'online thesaurus English' into a search engine to find an online thesaurus.

	Best option	**Alternative 1**	**Alternative 2**
to **participate** (2)	*to be a participant*	*to partake*	*to sit in on*
to **be the cause of** something (3)			
to **go along with** something (5)			
to **stay on track** (8)			
to **think through** an issue (9)			

5 **Optional extra: What other personality types do you find at meetings? For example, Michael Multitasker or Lesley Latecomer. Prepare a short description to present in the next session. Describe the person's character, how they behave at meetings and what effect they have on other participants and the meeting as a whole.**

› Language of meetings

1 Listen. Then read the dialogues with different partners.

B.11 **Dialogue 1**

A OK, let's get started. Is everyone happy with the minutes of the last meeting?
B Yes, they seem accurate to me.
A Great! Then let's get down to business.

B.12 **Dialogue 2**

B Can I just clarify the objective of today's meeting?
A Of course. The main aim of the meeting is to discuss the trainee programme.
B OK. Thanks for clarifying.
A So, let's kick things off.

B.13 **Dialogue 3**

A Sorry to cut you off but I don't think we have time to go into this now.
B OK, could we schedule a separate meeting to discuss it?
A Of course, so moving onto the next item. Paul, can you update us?
B Certainly!

B.14 **Dialogue 4**

A I think we've already covered this topic in enough detail. We can always come back to it later if there's time at the end.
B Sorry, you're right. We're running quite short on time.
A So, the next point we need to cover is costs. Can I hand over to you for this one, Ana?
B Yes, of course. Just a second. I just need to open the document.

B.15 **Dialogue 5**

A What's the latest on our partnership in Turkey?
B We've been making good progress.
A Have we signed the deal yet?
B Not quite, but we're close to a final agreement. So, things are looking good.

B.16 **Dialogue 6**

A Could you bring us up to speed on the product updates?
B Sure. Progress has been a bit slow, but we have trialled the beta version.
A When do you estimate the next version will be ready?
B If all goes according to plan, I'd guess it will be ready in a fortnight.

B.17 **Dialogue 7**

A I'm afraid that's all we have time for today.
B When's the next meeting?
A It's scheduled for the 18th. I'll send the minutes and action points round later today.
B Great, thank you.
A And thank you all for coming today. It was a very productive meeting. Is everyone happy with the action points we've agreed?
B Yes, I think so.
A OK. Then let's bring this meeting to a close.

2 In pairs. Practise new dialogues using alternative phrases. Take turns and change partners.

3 Focus on words: Find the word or phrase in the dialogues, which mean:

1. to explain or define something clearly
2. a goal or target
3. to open or begin (an informal term)
4. to interrupt a person who is speaking
5. to plan things for a particular time
6. to consider all the information about a topic
7. "There's not much time left."
8. "If everything happens the way we hope …"

4 Suggest another way of saying these phrases from the dialogues, without changing the meaning.

1. "The minutes seem accurate to me."
2. "Moving on to the next item."
3. "Can you update us, please?"
4. "We can come back to this later."
5. "Can I hand over to you?"
6. "We've been making good progress."
7. "The next meeting is scheduled for … "
8. "Let's bring this meeting to a close."

Tip

Add your own phrases to your *Essential phrases bank.*

5 Develop new dialogues, building on phrases from the Essential phrases bank on the right.

1. Choose one phrase from each category in the phrase bank. Mark it with a highlighter.
2. Work with a partner and develop new dialogues for each of these stages of a meeting, using your marked phrases.
   - Opening a meeting
   - Moving a topic on
   - Reporting on progress
   - Closing a meeting
3. Practise and perform your new dialogue(s) in class.

› Essential phrases

Opening a meeting

- Let's get started.
- Let's get down to business.
- Is everyone happy with the minutes of the last meeting?
- Can I just clarify the objective of today's meeting?
- The main aim of the meeting is to …
- So, let's kick things off.

Moving a topic on

- Sorry to cut you off but I don't think we have time to go into this now.
- We're running short on time.
- So, moving onto the next item.
- I think we've already covered this topic enough.
- We can come back to it later, if there's time (at the end).
- Can I hand over to you for this one / point / topic?
- So, the next point we need to cover is …

Reporting on progress

- Paul, can you update us?
- I have the latest … here.
- What's the latest on …?
- We've been making good progress.
- Progress has been a bit slow.
- Have we … yet?
- Not quite, but we're close to …
- Things are / aren't looking good / aren't looking too bad.
- Could you bring us up to speed on …?
- When do you estimate … will be ready?
- If all goes / If things go according to plan …,
- I'd guess it will be ready in a fortnight / by next month.

Closing a meeting

- I'm afraid that's all we have time for today.
- When's the next meeting?
- It's scheduled for …
- I'll send the minutes and action points round later today.
- Thank you all for coming today.
- Is everyone happy with the action points we've agreed (on)?
- Then let's bring this meeting to a close.

Session 1

1 Match the right answers to the questions on the left.

a) I was wondering whether you were free tomorrow morning?
b) Are you thinking about meeting online or in person?
c) Please let me know if you can make it.
d) Would it be possible to postpone our meeting by a day or two?
e) Can I give you a quick call about the agenda?

- [ ] That wouldn't be possible for me as I'll be on holiday then.
- [ ] I think we should meet in person.
- [ ] I'm busy until noon. Can you call me between 1 and 2 pm?
- [a] I'm afraid I'm not. How about the afternoon?
- [ ] I'm sorry but I can't. I already have a meeting planned.

2 Write a phrase with the same meaning as the one given.

I'm writing to confirm …	
	We'll be discussing …
	Please get back to me if …
Attached you will find …	
Kind regards,	

Session 2

1 Use a phrase from the list on the right to write a sentence for each of the scenarios below. There are two phrases you won't need.

› go on mute / mute your mics | book a meeting room | stop / interrupt someone | have trouble logging on | write something up ‹

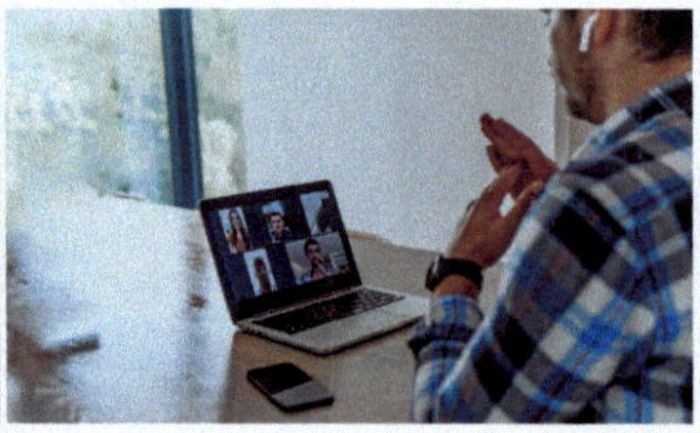

2 What can you say in a meeting …

a) … at the official beginning of a meeting?	
b) … to ask participants to focus and be brief?	
c) … to make sure participants know what the meeting is about?	
d) … to ask participants for regular updates?	
e) … at the end of a meeting?	

Session 3

1 Read the statements on the right. Then complete the minutes below with the passive form of the verbs used in the statements.

Team meeting Minutes
Date: 19/03 **Present:** AK, MG, BT, HS

1 Welcome
- Last meetings' minutes ____________________ by MG.
- This meetings' minutes ____________________ by AS.

2 Update on production and sales figures
- Good progress ________________ with the ramp up of production.
- More time ____________________ for the car park.
- Updates ____________________ by BT.
- Quarterly sales targets ____________________.

3 Outlook and action points
- Sales volumes ____________________.
- Suggestions ____________________ by the end of the week.

4 AOB
- Team outing ____________________ by BT.
- Ideas ____________________ to BT.

MG: First things first: I approve last meetings' minutes. Oh, Andreas, would you be so kind as to take the minutes for this meeting, please?

BT: We're making good progress with our production ramp up but we need more time for the additional car park. I'll send around updates on that by mail.

AK: So far, our sales are very slow. There is no way we'll reach our targets for this quarter.

MG: OK, we'll have to increase our sales volume. Mail me suggestions by the end of the week.

BT: Before I forget, send me your ideas for our next team outing. I'm organising that now.

B.18 **2 Read the statements below. Then listen to a podcast about virtual meetings and choose the correct words.**

a) Some people are **forced out of / fed up with / kept up with** any form of digital collaboration.
b) First of all, online meetings **require / reduce / request** travel and accommodation costs.
c) However, these meetings can potentially **relieve / deceive / decrease** overall productivity.
d) Online meetings pose **changes to effective / challenges in maintaining / chances for engaging** communication.

Business English *live*

1 Complete the phrases to match the responses.

A Could you bring ____?
B Sure. Renovation's completed. So far, the remodel of our main office is on schedule.

A Can I hand ____?
B Yes, of course. Our latest sales figures are looking good. We're on track to meet our targets.

A Could you just clarify ____?
B Sure, no problem. The aim of our meeting is to discuss and agree a new marketing strategy.

2 What can you say to …

a) begin a meeting? ______________________________
b) apologise for interrupting someone? ______________________________
c) briefly explain the objective of a meeting? ______________________________
d) express that not much progress has been made so far? ______________________________
e) stop any further discussion of a topic? ______________________________

THE BEST PLACE TO WORK

Remote working was often seen as a much sought after benefit that few people were offered prior to the 2020-2022 pandemic. Companies often feared a negative economic impact and refused requests to work from home. The pandemic made remote working the norm, but is it economically justified or just a modern convenience for workers? Here are two opposing opinions.

Marian Joyce

The office is dead Working in the office is an outdated tradition we no longer need. This is not just my personal opinion. It is backed up by top researchers at major universities such as Harvard and Stanford.

Research has proven that remote workers are around 35% more productive than office workers. Not only that, but they also make far fewer mistakes than office workers. If increased productivity and performance isn't enough to persuade you, then here are more reasons why it is better:

There are huge economic savings to be made by offering remote working. Just over 2% of all working hours are lost every year to sickness, but this rate is halved for remote workers. As a company, you are also much more likely to keep your employees if you offer more flexibility. Thus, saving a considerable amount of money on staff recruitment and training.

With happier, more productive and loyal staff, why would anyone want to go back to the office? And why should they?

Carl Mann

Happiness & the office After the 2020-22 pandemic many employees resisted returning to the office, but there are many reasons why we shouldn't give up on the office environment.

It may be harder to quantify in terms of productivity or attendance statistics, but what the office gives us is connections, engagement and a sense of purpose. Surveys frequently find that relationships with colleagues and managers are the top factors affecting job satisfaction. It can hardly be argued that these social benefits can be improved or even equalled by remote working.

What's more, these emotional connections can improve our health and wellbeing. Connections with others lead to increased personal happiness, better physical health and may even contribute to a longer life.

For ourselves, not for our bosses, I recommend that we embrace being in the office and the lifelong benefits it can provide us with.

Share

1 Before you read: Discuss these questions in class.

1. What's your organisation's policy on working from home?
2. Where can the tasks involved in your job be completed most effectively: at home or on your organisation's premises? Why?
3. How often do you work from home?
4. What are the main advantages and disadvantages of working from home in your opinion?

2 Read the text and answer the questions.

The office is dead

1. What are the main advantages of remote working in terms of productivity, according to Marian Joyce?
2. How can companies save money according to Joyce?
3. How do remote working employees feel, according to Joyce?

Happiness & the office

1. According to Carl, what is the main advantage of working in an office?
2. What two factors does he mention that can improve employee satisfaction?
3. What further benefits might people enjoy as a result of working in an office environment?

3 Suggest two more arguments of your own in favour of remote working.

1. ______________________________

2. ______________________________

4 Suggest two more arguments of your own in favour of working in the office.

1. ______________________________

2. ______________________________

5 Group discussion. Follow the instructions below and discuss the statement: 'Offices should be banned - everyone should work from home.'

1. Divide the class into two groups, A and B. Group A is in favour of remote working. Group B is in favour of working in the office.
2. Collect arguments in favour of your group's position. Refer back to the article and to your answers to tasks 3 or 4.
3. Consider arguments the other group might come up with. Find arguments to counter these. Refer back to the article and to your answers to tasks 3 or 4 for ideas.
4. Have a discussion in class. Make sure everyone has the chance to speak.

6 Your view. Write up the results of your discussion on remote working and working in the office in the style of meeting minutes.

NOT ANOTHER MEETING!

It's Sunday evening and you find yourself thinking about the working week ahead. As much as you try to stop the thoughts, you soon find yourself opening your calendar to see what the working week has in store. Monday is full of back-to-back meetings and the rest of the week isn't much better. Just when are you supposed to do some 'actual' work?

Life in the office can sometimes feel like one long meeting but some companies are putting into place policies to try to manage the situation. Shopify, the Canadian e-commerce company, started the New Year in 2023 by telling staff to cancel all recurring meetings with more than three people. Meetings were also banned on Wednesdays and meetings with more than 50 people could only happen on Thursdays between 11 am and 5 pm. Many other companies have also introduced 'no meeting days'.

The thought of banning meetings altogether may sound very attractive to many employees. However, in reality, meetings are necessary, if only to strengthen the feeling of belonging in a team. They just need to be made more effective. Here are some ideas for achieving this:

- ***Stop the meeting tourists*** Meetings should be limited to four or five people. When you have meetings with 20 or 30 people the majority of the attendees just sit there watching a few people talking.
- ***Ban recurring meetings*** Don't just have a team meeting at the same time every week because it's what you have always done. Instead, only meet when you have a specific task.
- ***Shorten meeting times*** Do you really need one hour, two hours or a whole morning? Reduce each meeting time by 25% to improve focus and efficiency.
- ***Don't always say yes*** Meeting overload can lead to employee stress and poor decision-making in meetings. Limiting the number of hours employees are allowed to spend in meetings each week can make employees feel valued, respected and in better control of their time.

As the saying goes 'Work smarter. Not harder.' So, perhaps the smartest decision meeting organisers could make would simply be to re-evaluate how, when and why they are holding a meeting, before sending out the meeting request!

Share

1 **Before you read: Read statements 1 - 4. Discuss your opinion on each statement with a partner.**

1 Meetings are often too long and not sufficiently focused.
2 Meetings are very important for team building.
3 The more people in a meeting, the less effective it is.
4 Problem solving and creativity are most effective in face-to-face meetings.

2 **Read the article. Which of the statements 1 - 4 in task 1 does the article support?**

3 **Read the text again and answer the questions.**

1. What do many working people do on a Sunday evening, according to the article?
2. What restrictions did *Shopify* introduce in terms of meetings in 2023?
3. If meetings were shorter, what might the effect be, according to the article?
4. What effect could limiting the number of meetings a person can attend have, according to the article?

4 **What do you understand by these terms? Explain them in your own words.**

1. back-to-back meetings
2. a meeting tourist
3. no meeting days
4. recurring meetings
5. meeting overload
6. Work smarter. Not harder.

5 **Which of the phenomena in task 4 have you experienced? Was the experience positive or negative? Why?**

6 **The article suggests four ideas for improving meeting effectiveness. Discuss the feasibility of each idea with a partner in the context of your own organisation.**

- Stop meeting tourists
- Ban recurring meetings
- Shorten meeting times
- Not always saying yes

7 **Suggest two more ideas of your own for improving the effectiveness of meetings in the context of your organisation. Compare your ideas with others in class. Use the ideas to create a five-point policy for more effective meetings in your workplace.**

Facts & stats

Agenda
- British & American numbering
- Complex numbers
- Talking about figures related to organisations
- Asking about figures related to organisations

a) twenty past ten

b) twenty after ten

a) nought to sixty mph

b) zero to sixty mph

a) half past six

b) half six

a) the fourth of December

b) April, twelve

a) nought point oh five

b) zero point zero five

a) two thousand ten

b) two thousand and ten

a) five hundred and fifty

b) five hundred fifty

› Small talk

Start the session by chatting with a partner about a recent sports or cultural event for a few minutes. Talk about when the event was, how many people you went with, how long the event was, etc. Your conversation can, of course, move on to other topics that come up naturally. Use the following phrases in your conversation.

Sounds amazing!

So what did you do after that?

Tip

A quick chat at the beginning of every English class is a great opportunity to practise and improve your small talk skills.

› Down to business

1 Discuss the following questions in class.

1. What kind of numbers do you find easiest and most problematic to say? Why?
   › Dates? | Years? | High numbers, e.g. over 100 or over 1,000,000? | Decimals? | ...? ‹
2. Look at the numbers in the collage above: Both ways of saying each are correct, but which version, a) or b), would you usually use?
3. Which version a) or b) is typically British, typically American or typical of both American and British English, do you think?

› p. 4 in digital module 1.1.C

2a Look at the statistics below. Take turns in class to read out a sentence: speak slowly and clearly and focus on saying the figures correctly.

Did you know?

71% of small-to-mid-sized businesses use social media.

73% of people surveyed wouldn't care if the brands they use disappeared from their life.

LinkedIn now has more than 900 million members with over 58 million registered companies.

1 in 10 people born in Europe are conceived in an **IKEA** bed.

The red and white Coca-Cola logo is recognised by 94% of the world's population.

There are about 582 million entrepreneurs on the earth.

The game **Candy Crush** brings in more than $633,000 in revenue every day.

Around 50% of small businesses start at home.

Every **Apple iPhone** ad displays the time 9:41 AM, the time Steve Jobs unveiled it in 2007.

If Bill Gates were a country, he'd be the 37th richest country on earth.

2b Answer the questions.

1. Which of the statistics do you find surprising? Which do you find impressive? Why?
2. What kinds of numbers do you work with in your daily work?
3. How big a role do numbers play in your job?
4. Do you know any interesting facts or figures?

C.01 **3a** Listen to a podcast interview with Leah, the co-founder of a sportswear company. Note down as many facts and stats as you can.

3b Team up with a partner and compare your notes.

C.01 **3c** Now listen again and take notes on the following points:

- The inspiration behind the company
- Where GreenFit operates
- The kind of products they offer
- GreenFit's commitment to all areas of sport

Leah, co-founder of GreenFit

› p. 5 in digital module 1.1.C

4a **Prepare to talk to other students in class about your organisation (or an organisation you know). First add the missing words to these questions.**

1. When ________ the organisation founded?
2. How many employees ________ the organisation currently have?
3. How much ________ spent on sponsorship by the organisation every year?
4. How high ________ the organisation's sales figures last year?

4b **Answer the questions in 4a by completing sentences 1 - 4 below. Use a different word from the options provided and add an appropriate figure each time.**

› approximately | almost | over | nearly | around ‹

1. I'm not sure, but I think it was founded in ________________________.
2. As far as I know, we now have ________________________ employees.
3. I'm not certain, but I think ________________________ Euros / Dollars was spent on sponsorship last year.
4. If I remember rightly, sales figures were ________________________ last year.

4c **Now carry out a 'Find someone who' survey in class. Ask people in class the questions in 4a and find at least one person for each point. Use phrases and ideas from 4b when you give your answers.**

Find someone who knows ...

... when their company was founded.

... the number of employees their company has.

... how much their company spends on sponsorship of teams / clubs / events.

... what the last year's sales figures of their company was.

4d **What did you find out? Tell the class the most interesting fact that you found out.**

5a **Finding out more. Work in pairs, write questions with *what, how many, where, when,* and *how much*, to elicit the information given in the short company profiles at the top of the next page.**

ENERGIZER

Enjoy watching this video clip.

C.1

5b **Practise talking about the companies with your partner. One of you works for *Soledad Bank*, the other for *Ecopower*. Take turns to ask and answer your questions from 5a.**

SOLEDAD BANK	ECOPOWER - Renewable Energy
Main office in Bogota	Headquarters in Oslo, Norway
1,800 branches in South America	Founded 1994
23,500 employees worldwide	18 solar farms, 60 wind farms
46 overseas branches	1,500 employees worldwide
36,000,000 account holders	Annual turnover €525,000,000
Annual turnover $1,750,000,000	Current share price €64.20

6a **Work with a new partner. One of you works for Company A, the other for Company B. Give your company a name and add appropriate figures to the profiles. Don't show your partner your figures.**

1 Company name
2 Place name
3 Year
4 Number over 1,000
5 Number under 100
6 Figure in dollars
7 Number over a million

A

(1) ____________________

Manufacturer of packaging machines

Founded in (2) ____________

in (3) ____________________

(4) ______________ employees

(5) ______________ subsidiaries outside of Europe

Current share price (6) __________

B

(1) ____________________

Streaming platform

based in (2) ____________

Founded (3) ____________

(4) ______________ users

Current share price (6) __________

Annual turnover (7) __________

6b **Role play: You meet your partner at an international convention and make small talk about your companies (A and B) after one of the sessions. Ask your partner questions to find out about their company and add the missing information. Make sure you have a conversation, not an interview.**

› Review and AOB

Review what you have learned in this session:

1. Give examples to show how American and British English differ when saying a date, a time and high numbers.
2. Give examples of three important statistics about your organisation or an organisation you know.
3. Suggest three questions you could ask someone about their company.

› Final feedback

What did you find most useful in this session? Tell the class. Any questions?

› p. 7 in digital module 1.1.C

1 **Read the interview with the founder of a bicycle company.**

Business Impact

Q & A
Making an impact

In this months' *Making an Impact Q&A,* we talk to Sepp Thomas, co-founder of SELA Bikes on their beginnings and the journey so far.

When did you start the company and what was your motivation? I have always loved cycling. Growing up here in Boulder, Colorado, I was surrounded by mountains and bikes. As a kid, I basically just rode my bike, watched cycling on TV, and fixed up old bikes with my best friend Larry. And when I realised I was never going to ride the *Tour de France,* I decided to focus on the bikes themselves. I started the company in 2002 with Larry, working out of his garage. It was cool, but there was barely room to swing a cat in there.

» *The last time I checked, we had 1.3 million followers*

Well, you are no longer in Larry's garage. How has the company grown over the years? It's been amazing, to be honest. We sold 13 bikes in our first year, but from those humble beginnings, we now have over 75,000 customers worldwide and our annual revenue rose to almost $37 million last year.

I suppose you are no longer making all of these bikes yourself. How many employees does the company have? No! If it were only me, we'd probably sell about 5 bikes a year. Thankfully we have grown to 185 employees, who are spread over 26 stores all over the world and our main offices here in Colorado and in Amsterdam. That also includes our technicians and sales team.

Let's talk bikes. What do you specialise in and what are your bestsellers? We started by producing high-end carbon road bikes as that was our passion. This is still a huge part of our identity here, but we have expanded our range greatly, to almost 70 products, including children's bikes, touring bikes, mountain bikes and cargo bikes. And in recent years, the massive increase in demand for e-bikes has been a game changer.

What is the price range of your bikes? Standard bikes for children and adults start at $350 and our most-expensive carbon road bike, the SELA Pelaton, currently costs $12,999, and if you want to go custom-made, the sky's the limit. Our e-bikes sell for between $1,850 and $7,500.

When did you branch out into clothing? We designed and produced our first cycling jerseys in 2021 and we now have a wide range of cycling clothing and accessories, as well as casual clothing. In fact, last year we sold almost 32,000 items. Fashion is very important to cycling and we wanted to provide stylish clothing to complement our beautiful bikes.

Tell us about the role of the internet and social media in your company's growth. Online retail has been a significant focus for us. We revamped our website, and our e-commerce platform now serves over 75% of our customers. We also have a strong presence on social media. The last time I checked, we had 1.3 million followers on Instagram. Not bad for a couple of guys messing around with bikes in a garage!

Magazine

2 **What do the figures in the article refer to? Note down the reference and the figure.**

Reference	Figure
Number of followers	*1.3 million*

3 **What do you think the underlined terms and expressions mean? Have a guess, before checking in an online dictionary.**

a) "It was cool, but there was barely room to swing a cat in there."

b) "From those humble beginnings, we now have over 75,000 customers."

c) "... the massive increase in demand for e-bikes has been a game changer."

d) "... if you want to go custom-made, the sky's the limit."

4 **Suggest a less idiomatic alternative for each of the sentences in task 3, keeping the same meaning, but not using the underlined expressions.**

a) ______

b) ______

c) ______

d) ______

5 **Optional extra: Summarise the interview as a report, focussing on the facts and figures. Be prepared to present your report in the next session.**

› p. 9 in digital module 1.1.C

Ups & Downs

Agenda
- Talking about numbers, statistics & figures
- Describing positive & negative change
- Understanding & describing graphs & charts

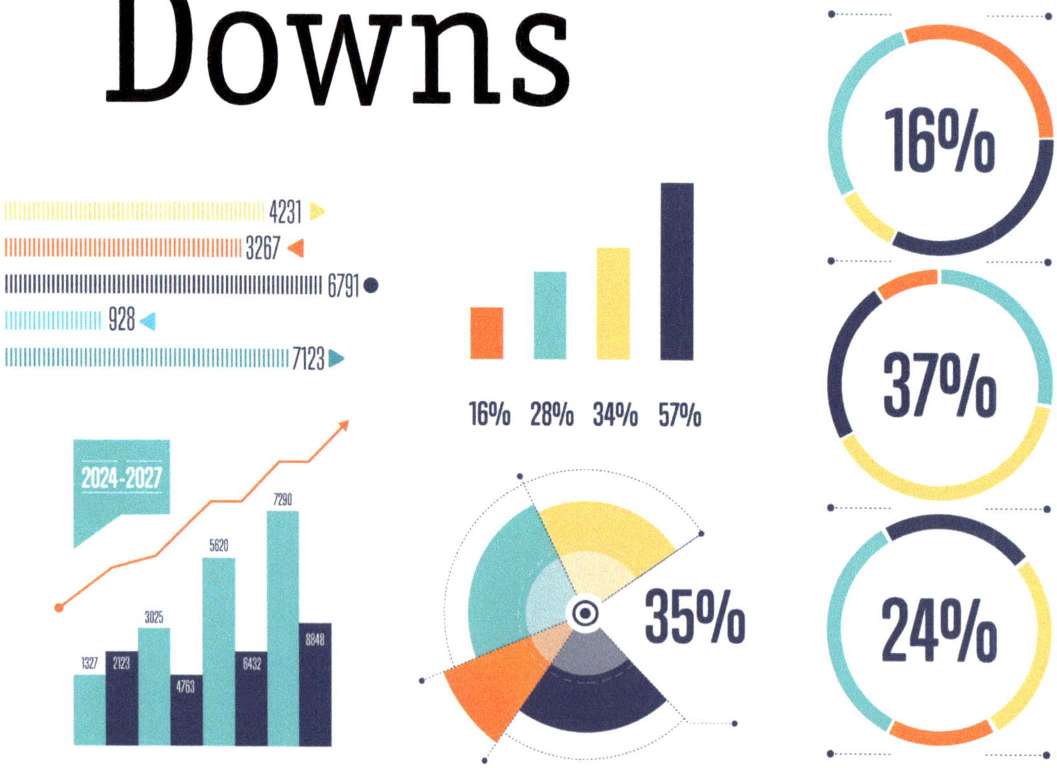

› Small talk

Start the session by chatting with a partner for a few minutes about a film or series that you have recently watched. Your conversation can, of course, move on to other topics that come up naturally. Use the phrases on the right in your conversation.

Have you ever seen …?

What's that about?

› Down to business

1 Discuss the following questions in class

1. Are you a 'numbers person'? Why / why not? What does it mean to be a 'numbers person'?
2. How do you prefer to read about trends: in articles and texts, or in charts and diagrams? Why?
3. What kind of statistics do you regularly come across either in your line of work or in your private life?

2a Read the four short news stories. Which describe a positive and which a negative change?

1

K-Play reaches new heights as competitor struggles

Seoul Korean streaming platform *K-Play* has seen a surge in users over the last six months, growing from 110,000,000 to almost 125,000,000. The platform's extensive library of high-quality content and the collapse of its US rival *Dreamstream* have helped *K-Play*. *(jk)*

2

Raising awareness and profits

London The sports company *GreenFit* is using a new range of sports clothes to raise awareness about climate change. The *Pro Planet* range aims to reduce the company's carbon footprint and increase consumer interest in protecting the environment and slowing down climate change. *(lm)*

3

Germany's decline continues

Berlin Germany slipped to 27th in the world rankings after their dramatic 5-1 collapse against England last night. This was the perfect end to a terrible year for the national team as performances steadily worsened and attendances fell to an average of just over 30,000. England's 7th victory in a row sees them climb to 3rd in the world rankings. *(kr)*

4

Crunch time for Soledad Bank as interest rates continue to rise

Bogota The current unstable financial landscape has caused a downturn in the fortunes of the *Soledad Bank*. A rise in interest rates and increased costs have led to a sharp reduction in consumer borrowing. Financial experts do not expect this downward trend to change anytime soon. *(sy)*

2b Find the words and expressions in the articles with the same meanings as those given below.

Article 1

1. a sudden increase ____________
2. a sudden failure ____________

Article 2

3. to increase ____________
4. to make something happen more slowly ____________

Article 3

5. to fall or slide downwards ____________
6. to get worse and worse ____________

Article 4

7. a decline in the amount of something ____________
8. a large fall ____________

2c Start a 'Describing change' phrase bank with the words and phrases from 2b. Then add more words from the article and words that you know.

Describing change phrase bank

surge = sudden increase

2d Compare your phrase bank with a partner and exchange useful words.

› p. 11 in digital module 1.1.C

3a *raise or rise*? **Both verbs mean 'increase', but when do you use which one? Decide whether you think** ***raise*** **or** ***rise*** **is correct in the following sentences. Then check in class.**

1. The company used the event to ________________ money for a local charity.
2. Costs are ________________ and this has affected many people.
3. The demand for electric vehicles has ________________ steadily in recent years.
4. The fans were angry after the club decided to ________________ ticket prices for the new season.

3b Read the explanations. Decide which sentence applies to which verb. Add the missing information.

1. **raise | rise** is a regular verb. The three forms are: ________________
2. **raise | rise** is an irregular verb. The three forms are: ________________
3. **raise | rise** always has an object. The company has ____________ prices again.
4. **raise | rise** doesn't need an object. Costs have ____________ by 6%.

3c Write four more sentences of your own: Two using 'rise' and two using 'raise'. Read your sentences in class and check that everyone has used the verbs correctly.

Tip

When you read out your sentences, say 'beep' instead of 'rise' or 'raise'. The other students must say which verb is missing.

A The price of oil has *beep* by 5%.
B The price of oil has *risen* by 5%.

rise

1. ________________
2. ________________

raise

1. ________________
2. ________________

ENERGIZER

Enjoy watching this video clip.

C.2

4a Graphs and charts are effective visual ways of showing figures and statistics to make them more easily understandable. Which three kinds of charts are shown below? Choose the correct name from the selection offered.

› bar chart | line chart | area graph | pie chart | venn diagram or graph ‹

a) 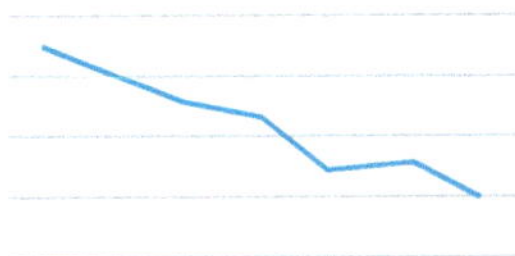

b) 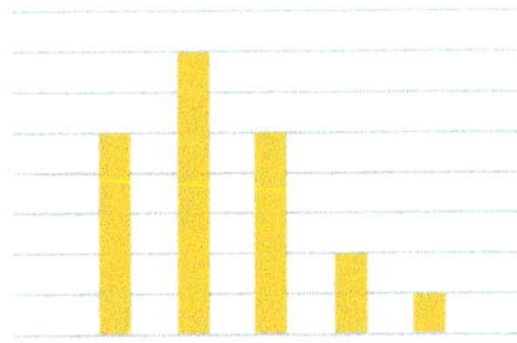

c) 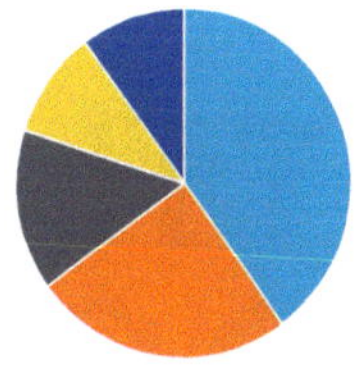

d) 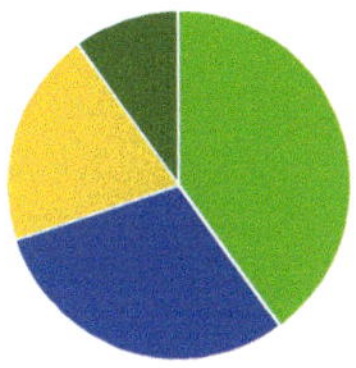

e) 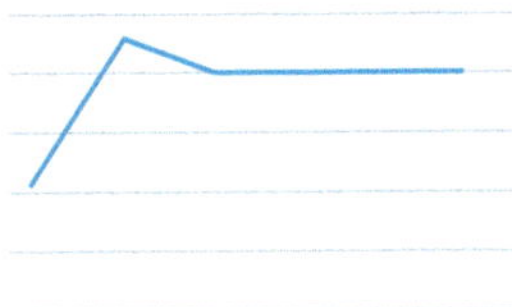

f) 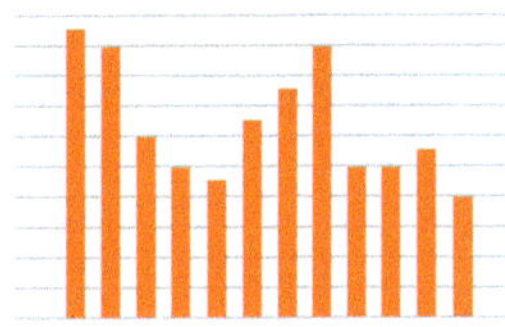

4b Draw a simple diagram illustrating the two other kinds of graphs named in the selection.

5a Listen to six short audios and decide which audio 1 - 6 matches which graph or chart a - f.

C.02-04 **1.** Graph / Chart: ☐ **2.** Graph / Chart: ☐ **3.** Graph / Chart: ☐

C.05-07 **4.** Graph / Chart: ☐ **5.** Graph / Chart: ☐ **6.** Graph / Chart: ☐

5b Practise talking about figures and statistics.

1. Choose one of the following topics and think about the ups and downs, highs and lows, etc. for you. Decide which type of diagram you think would best illustrate the topic and draw your visual.
   › My typical working day | My typical working week | My typical year | My typical weekend ‹
2. Now talk to a partner but don't show him / her your graph. Take it in turns to describe your graph to your partner. Choose expressions from your 'Describing change' phrase bank. Your partner should try and draw a graph matching what you say.
3. Show each other your graphs. Whose graph is most accurate?
4. Choose a different topic and different kind of chart and repeat the exercise with a different partner.

› Review and AOB

Review what you have learned in this session:

1. Suggest three words for upward and downward movement.
2. Explain the difference between *rise* and *raise* and give an example using each.
3. Name three different kinds of charts and suggest when you might use them in your daily work.

› Final feedback

What did you find most useful in this session? Tell the class. Any questions?

 › p. 13 in digital module 1.1.C

1 **Read the article about misleading graphs and charts.**

Business Impact

THE NUMBERS DON'T LIE

..., do they?

We come across charts and graphs in many areas of our daily life – at work, on the news, on social media, when we watch sport, just to name a few. Charts and graphs are useful for showing data, and helping people explain and understand larger or more complex issues. However, they can sometimes trick you. Let's look at some ways they can be misleading.

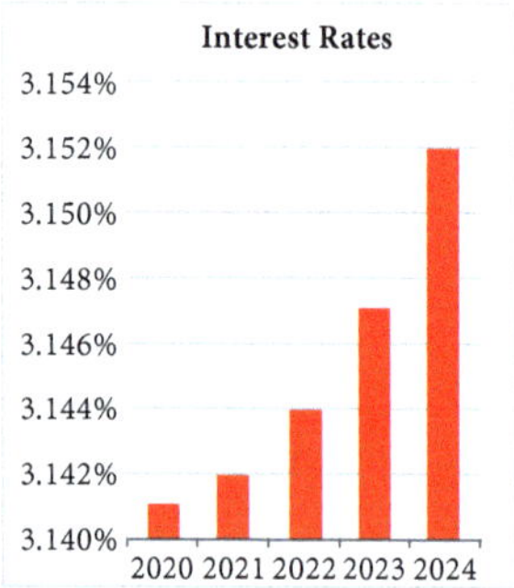

1. Changing the Scale

Graphs can fool you by making small differences look big or hiding important changes. For example, a bar chart might start at a number above zero, making small changes appear much larger.

2. Picking Data Wisely

Sometimes, people only show part of the data, leaving out information that doesn't support their point. For example, a company might show a line chart for a stock's performance but skip the months when the price dropped a lot. This is known as cherry picking.

3. Using Strange Scales

Fancy 3D or weird scales in charts can make it hard to understand the data. A 3D bar chart can make comparisons difficult because the height, width and depth all affect what you see. By making a piece of the pie look bigger, it can appear more important or impressive than something with the same size or value.

4. Unclear Labels and Titles

Charts can be confusing when the labels or titles are unclear. If you don't know what each part of the chart means, you might get the wrong idea. If you want to avoid being fooled, then remember:
› Check the scale on the chart's axes.
› Look for missing data and ask for the full story.
› Be cautious with 3D effects and strange scales.
› Make sure the labels and legends are clear.

Whatever graph or chart you are looking at, always look with a critical eye and pay attention to the details. This way, you'll recognise deceptive charts and you'll understand the information better.

Magazine

› p. 14 in digital module 1.1.C

2 **Answer the questions. Find the answers in the article.**

a) Why can it be misleading if the scale on a chart doesn't start at zero?

____

b) What is meant by the term 'cherry picking'?

____

c) If you want one aspect in a chart to look more impressive, what could you do?

____

d) Why are labels and titles important on charts?

____

3 **Which of the tips to avoid being fooled is most important in your opinion? Come up with one more tip in the same style.**

4 **Focus on words: Find these words and expressions in the article, then explain them in your own words and add the meaning in your language.**

a) complex issues ____________________

b) to support a point ____________________

c) to skip something ____________________

d) to get the wrong idea ____________________

e) axis (plural axes) ____________________

f) legend ____________________

5 **Compare the graphs in the article, both of which display the same information in different ways. Answer the questions and be prepared to share your ideas in the next session.**

a) What did the person who created each graph want to express?

b) Why might both charts be misleading?

c) Who might benefit from each representation?

6 **Optional extra: Look at the chart and write a short text to explain what is shown. Then, just for fun, create your own chart that represents your job or your daily life. Make notes explaining your chart and be prepared to present your chart to the class in the next session.**

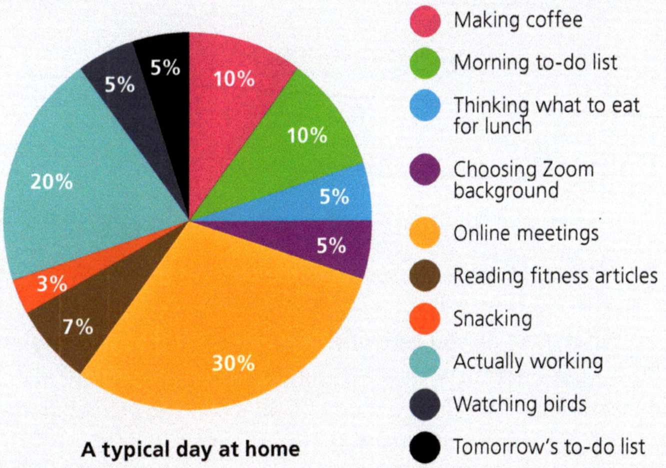

A typical day at home

Agenda
- Talking about goals
- Talking about the future
- Understanding the difference between *will* & *going to* future

Looking *ahead*

› Small talk

Start the session by chatting with a partner for a few minutes about what you do in your free time and any hobbies you have. Your conversation can, of course, move on to other topics that come up naturally. Use the following phrases in your conversation.

That's really unusual!

Have you ever tried … ?

› Down to business

1 Discuss the following questions in class.

1. Which goals are represented in the pictures above? Which of them might you consider or have you achieved in your life?
2. What goals do you currently have with regard to your professional and / or personal life?
3. In your opinion, what are the pros and cons of setting goals?
4. How important do you think it is for a company to set goals, for the organisation as a whole and for teams and individual members of staff?

› p. 16 in digital module 1.1.C

C.08 **2a** You are going to listen to a podcast interview in which Leah, co-founder of the sportswear company, *GreenFit*, talks about the company's future plans. Listen to the podcast for the first time and note down information about *GreenFit's* plans in the four key areas covered in the interview:

Retail Stores

Employees

Sustainability

Product Range

2b Team up with two other members of your class and compare the information you have noted down. Add any information you have missed. You can make notes here:

3a As a team, use your notes from 2a and prepare a report on *GreenFit's* future plans to present to your class. If possible, add a diagram or chart to illustrate each topic. Each person in your team should be prepared to present at least one of the topics.

3b Practise, then present your reports to the class, using your notes and your charts.

ENERGIZER

Enjoy watching this video clip.

C.3

› p. 17 in digital module 1.1.C

4a Focus on the future: Sentences 1 - 12 are all sentences used by Leah to talk about *GreenFit's* future plans. Read the sentences and discuss in class which tense of the verb in brackets you think was used in each sentence. Don't add the verb unless you are really certain!

1. (aim to) In the next five years we ________________ open 50 new retail outlets.
2. (cover) This investment ________________ not only the new stores but also further development of our existing locations.
3. (contribute to) We're confident that this ________________ a substantial revenue increase in the coming years.
4. (plan to) Over the next three years, we ________________ introduce 150 new products …
5. (focus on) … and we ________________ some new sports.
6. (plan to) We also ________________ introduce new sustainable materials for our sportswear.
7. (plan to) By 2025, we ________________ reduce our overall carbon emissions by 40%.
8. (be | succeed) It ________________ a challenge, but I am confident we ________________ .
9. (spend) Over the next five years, we ________________ around €80 million on these sustainability initiatives.
10. (need to) We ________________ hire more talent.
11. (plan to) We ________________ add between 400 and 500 employees to our workforce over the next three years.
12. (find) I just hope we ________________ the right people.

C.08 **4b Now listen to the interview again and add the missing verbs.**

5a Focus on function, tense and verb: Look at the functions and examples below. Add the tense used in each case.

› simple present | *going to* future | *will* future ‹

	Function	Example	Tense
1.	to refer to things that will (not) happen with certainty and are unchangeable	Prices will rise by 10% next year.	*will-future*
2.	to refer to things that you hope, think or expect to happen	I hope prices won't increase next year.	________________
3.	to refer to things that have been planned already	They're going to increase prices next year.	________________
4.	to refer to future plans using a verb of planning (aim, plan, intend, propose)	They plan to increase prices next year.	________________

5b Now look at the sentences in 4a again. Match each sentence to its function and crosscheck the tense used.

6a **Write four sentences about your expectations for the future using the prompts given.**

In the near future, I hope I will …

By (year) I'm confident I will …

In five years, I think I will …

With any luck, at some time in the future I will …

Tip
Always use the *will* future for future expectations.

6b **Now chat with a partner: How similar or different are your expectations?**

7a **Now write four sentences about things you have planned for the coming week. Two sentences should be true and two should be false.**

Tip
Always use 'going to', the present progressive or a verb of planning in the present tense for things you've planned.

7b **Work with a partner and take turns to read out your sentences. Try to guess which sentences are true and which are false.**

"Actually, it's not my business plan. It's my plan for planning a plan."

Review and AOB

Review what you have learned in this session:

1. Suggest three goals for the week ahead.
2. Give three examples of future plans showing you know when to use the *will* future
3. Give three examples of future plans showing you know when to use 'going to'.

Final feedback

What did you find most useful in this session? Tell the class. Any questions?

› p. 19 in digital module 1.1.C

1 Read the article about future trends.

WHAT DOES *the future hold?*

We asked four experts to tell us what life in the future could look like in four key areas: business, work, travel and health. Here's what they had to say.

BUSINESS | Valerie Oliviera, business analyst

In the world of business, it's likely that technology will keep evolving at a rapid pace, revolutionising the way companies operate. We can expect a surge in data-driven decision-making, as analytics becomes essential to business strategies. The adoption of AI and automation is sure to transform workflows, enhancing productivity and hopefully creating new job opportunities. Maybe in the next few years, companies can find a way to make money without destroying the planet.

WORK | Jane Wednesday, founder of *Career Vision*

We definitely predict that remote and flexible jobs will become more common, as companies embrace this trend. More people will have the opportunity to work from home, and this might improve their work-life balance. We also hope that this will lead to greater workforce diversity. However, it might not always be easy to manage teams of people who work from different places, and some companies will face challenges. Unfortunately, we expect there will still be some obstacles for mothers and single parents to successfully combine looking after their children with continuing their career.

TRAVEL | Dr Eliza Schmidt, university professor

It's quite likely that electric vehicles will become more affordable and more widespread. I also predict an increase in people using e-bikes and e-scooters to get to work and school, especially in larger cities where roads have become more dangerous and parking either impossible or very expensive. I hope that more cities will invest in better public transport, bike lanes and safer areas for walking, as all of these can help reduce traffic congestion by encouraging people to leave their cars at home. However, I am certain that there will still be many people who choose to drive everywhere because it is so convenient or the public transport is too unreliable. I really hope that fewer people will choose to fly long distances on holidays as the issue of climate change and sustainability become more important.

HEALTH | Andre Milner, fitness trainer

I believe that people will become more interested in maintaining their overall health. Regular exercise, meditation and healthy eating habits such as veganism will become more common. I am confident that this shift towards a healthier lifestyle will lead to a happier and more energetic society. I also predict that technology will continue to play a bigger role in supporting our health and fitness goals, making it easier for individuals to monitor their well-being. However, there will definitely be challenges, such as finding the time and motivation to stay active and eat healthily when you have a busy life.

2 Write one or two sentences summarising each expert's most important predictions.

a) Valerie Oliviera: ______________________________

____

b) Jane Wednesday: ______________________________

____

c) Dr Eliza Schmidt: ______________________________

____

d) Andre Milner: ______________________________

____

3 Focus on words: Find the terms used in the article with these meanings:

Valeria Oliviera
a) decisions made according to information that has been collected
b) to change the way people work or work processes are organised

Jane Wednesday
c) to accept a new idea
d) to have to deal with difficult new concepts

Dr Eliza Schmidt
e) existing in many places, common
f) to put money into something to make a profit

Andre Milner
g) a (slight) change in direction
h) state of feeling happy and healthy

Business Impact

Defining and paraphrasing words or expressions is a useful skill when you don't know the exact term or when a person asks you to explain something:
It refers to …
It means the same as …
It's the opposite of …
It's a type of … that …
It's a person who …

4 Find four more words or expressions in the article which you would like to use in future. Note them down and 'paraphrase' their meaning for someone who doesn't understand them.

5 Choose one of the people in the article and write what the person says in your own language, following steps a), b) and c).

a) Create a version of your own without any help from a dictionary or online translator.
b) Enter the original text into an online translator of your choice and compare the translation with your own version.
c) Create a 'best' version from your own and the online version.

Tip

Enter 'translate English' into a search engine to find an online translator. Try different online translators to see which you find most reliable.

6 Optional extra: Choose one of the topics below and write your own short text about the future. Include what you hope, think and believe will and will not happen. Be prepared to present your text in the next session.

› Your organisation / job | Your hometown or region | Your country ‹

› Talking numbers & figures

1 Listen. Then read the dialogues with different partners.

C.09 **Dialogue 1**

A When was your company founded?
B We started up in 2019 with just a handful of employees.
A And how many people are employed there now?
B I don't know the exact number, but I think around approximately 2,500.

C.10 **Dialogue 2**

A How big is the company now? I mean, has the company grown over the last five years or so?
B We're seeing steady growth. We now have over 750,000 customers worldwide.
A That sounds like a good number to me.
B Yes, and our annual revenue rose to almost $37 million last year.

C.11 **Dialogue 3**

A What effect has the economic crisis had on your company?
B We've seen a reduction in turnover of 3.7% and around a fifth of the workforce was on short-time work for around six months.
A That doesn't sound good.
B No, it wasn't good. But things are picking up again. We had a small increase in turnover of 0.7% in the last quarter and we're confident things will pick up again in the new year.
A That's good news then.

C.12 **Dialogue 4**

A Does your company have any sustainability targets for the future?
B Yes, of course. We're planning to reduce carbon emissions by at least a third across all areas.
A And what kind of timescale are we talking about here?
B Well, we're aiming high and we hope to achieve our goal within the next three years.

C.13 **Dialogue 5**

A What are your goals moving forward?
B We want to expand. Over the next five years, we aim to open up to ten new stores across Europe.
A What about employee growth? Will you be expanding your team further?
B Absolutely! We're planning to add between 30 and 50 new employees to our workforce over the next three to five years.

C.14 **Dialogue 6**

A Why have you decided to raise prices next year?
B Unfortunately, due to circumstances beyond our control, our costs have almost doubled, so we had no choice in the matter.
A So how much will you be raising prices by?
B The prices for most goods will only rise by about 10%, but in some cases it could be substantially more.

2 In pairs. Practise new dialogues using alternative phrases. Take turns and change partners.

3 **Focus on words: Find the word or phrase in the dialogues, which means:**

1. a small number

____

2. a high figure

____

3. out of our control

____

4. a lot more

____

5. the time in which something happens

____

6. not working full time because of a crisis

____

4 **Search for further words or phrases in the dialogues for each category in the Essential phrases bank on the right. Then come up with a new idea for each category based on your organisation.**

5 **In pairs. Use the questions in the dialogues to ask a partner about their company. Change questions to suit the organisation and situation.**

6 **Change partners. Choose one of the dialogues and continue the conversation with your own ideas.**

7 **Develop new dialogues, building on phrases from the Essential phrases bank.**

1. Choose one phrase from each category in the phrase bank. Mark it with a highlighter.
2. Work with a partner and develop new dialogues using your marked phrases.
3. Practise and perform your new dialogue(s) in class.

› Essential phrases

Useful questions

- When was the company founded?
- How many people are employed there?
- How big is the company?
- Has the company grown over the last ten years?
- Why have you decided to (raise prices)?
- How much will you be (raising prices by)?
- What kind of timescale are we talking about here?
- What are your goals moving forward?
- What effect has the economic crisis had on your company?

Reporting on development

- We're seeing steady growth.
- The company has grown over recent years.
- Our annual revenue rose to (almost $37 million last year).
- Costs have almost doubled.
- Turnover has risen / fallen by (€3.5 million).

Essential verbs

- to achieve a goal (within a certain time)
- to add
- to aim high
- to be founded (The company was founded in …)
- to double (Prices have doubled.)
- to expand
- to grow by (ten percent) / to increase by (ten percent)
- to pick up
- to raise (prices by …)
- to reduce
- to rise
- to see a reduction (in turnover)
- to see steady growth
- to start up (We started up in …)

Essential expressions

- a good number (That sounds like a good number to me.)
- a handful
- a small increase (in prices) / an increase by (ten percent)
- a third / a quarter / a fifth
- almost / around / approximately (I think around approximately 2,500.)
- at least
- over the next five years
- the exact number (I don't know the exact number.)
- Due to circumstances beyond our control.
- We had no choice in the matter.
- That's good news then!

Session 1

C.15

1 Listen to the newscast and complete the gaps.

***ShipAI's* financial performance impressive**

ShipAI has delivered a stellar performance in the latest financial quarter. When an ________ increase in annual revenue became public, the company's share price almost ________. Net profits have gone up sharply to reach ________. This quarter has been the fourth best in the company's history.

ShipAI's net profit margin stood at a robust 17.5% and the number of its clients has grown by about ________. In a labour market where highly skilled workers are increasingly rare, its workforce has expanded to a total of ________ employees with about ________ coming from under-represented groups. Average salaries at *ShipAI* have risen by ________ in the last 5 years. *ShipAI* is raising its dividend to ________ cents a share.

2 Find and write the terms from the text with the same meaning.

a) ________ a number over half a billion euros
b) ________ 40%
c) ________ 20%
d) ________ gone up by twice as much
e) ________ 33%

Session 2

1 Read the descriptions a), b) and c). Now look at the charts and write the correct number in the boxes.

a) a state of affairs at a specific time
b) two trends over time
c) a comparison between different items at a specific time

☐

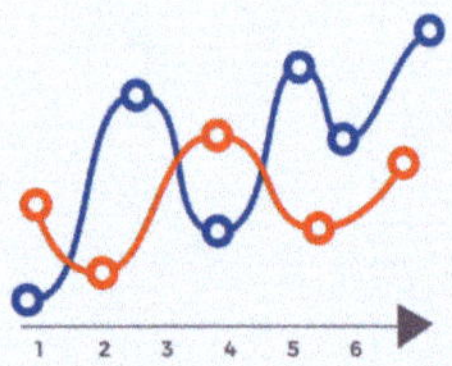

____

☐

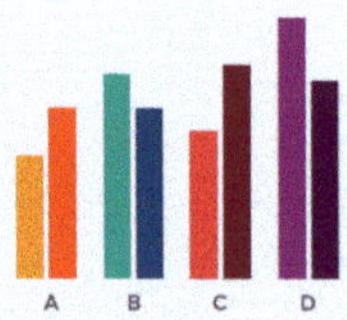

____

☐

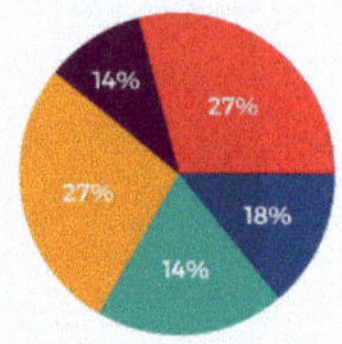

____

2 Write the name of the chart under the graphs.

3 Read the statements below and cross out the wrong option.

a) Heating has become more expensive as energy prices have **raised / risen** so much.
b) Our company is making more money this year because it **rose / raised** prices last year.
c) The demand for e-cars is expected to **surge / decline** further as sales volumes keep growing.
d) The value of cryptocurrency has **risen / raised** so much that is **raises / rises** fears of a crash.
e) Sponsorship of this athlete had already **raised / slowed down** but this latest scandal has led to a sharp **decline / surge** of it.

Session 3

1 Find an appropriate ending for each sentence.

a) In order to be more confident at meetings,
b) I was asked if I wanted to work full-time instead of part-time
c) The company is likely to relocate within the next year
d) My colleague's been promoted to team leader
e) There is a job opening in the marketing department and

☐ and maybe I will.
☐ she's planning to apply for it.
☐ and plans to reduce the staff.
☐ I'm going to take a class to improve my public speaking skills.
☐ so many employees will have to move.

2 Give short answers to the following questions.

a) Will prices continue to go up? No, ______________________.
b) Are you going to visit our headquarters? No, ______________________.
c) Does he plan to hire employees? No, ______________________.
d) Do they aim to enter the French market? No, ______________________.
e) Are you all staying in a hotel? No, ______________________.

Business English live

1 Find the odd one out.

a) grow / add / rise / reduce
b) a third / a half / quarterly / a fifth
c) substantial / surge / steady / sharp
d) exactly / around / almost / approximately

2 Choose the best answer.

a) Have you decided whether to raise prices next year?
☐ Prices will probably rise by 5% over the year.
☐ Yes, we're going to raise prices by 5% at the beginning of the year.
☐ Yes, we will. We'll keep prices steady.

b) What effect has the economic crisis had on your company?
☐ Well, our turnover has risen by half.
☐ Well, our turnover has doubled.
☐ Well, our turnover has been reduced by half.

c) What are your goals moving forward?
☐ Over the next three years we want to expand.
☐ For the last five years we have expanded.
☐ Business is steady so we're satisfied.

d) Will you be expanding your workforce?
☐ Yes, we might have to let some people go, unfortunately.
☐ Yes, we want to raise prices.
☐ Yes, we're aiming to increase our headcount by 20% this year.

ARE WE DROWNING IN A SEA OF NUMBERS?

In today's world, we see lots of numbers and statistics everywhere. They can help us make choices and understand things. But do we have too many numbers in our lives, and do statistics have too great an influence on us? Find out what two experts think.

James Roberts

YES

James Roberts, sociology professor Numbers are overwhelming us. Day after day, we spend hours tracking walks and runs, counting calories, checking our bank balance, comparing prices and studying league tables.

In my opinion, the constant flow of statistics in news, social media and advertising is just too much to take in. On top of that, how are we supposed to know what information we can trust? I understand that statistics can be a useful tool to explain things, but we are seeing more and more fake statistics, and not everyone is in a position to judge what's true. This can lead to bad choices, fear, and distrust.

I am also worried that the more we focus on numbers and statistics, the less we focus on the people behind the numbers. I don't want to live in a world where emotions and personal relationships are less important than a set of numbers. Our obsession with numbers is just another example of people losing touch with the real world - the 'live' world. Instead, we're drowning in the digital world.

However, my biggest fear is the effect this is having on people. If people have too much exposure to statistics, especially to negative ones, it can lead to anxiety and stress. Constantly hearing about risks, crises and negative trends can have a negative influence on our mental well-being.

And if we become more focused on measurable achievements, such as performance, wealth and productivity, then we might forget about qualities such as personal growth and kindness. You cannot measure happiness with numbers.

Dr Emma Pearson

NO

Dr Emma Pearson Numbers help us make better decisions. We now live in a world with masses of information, and statistics help us make sense of it. We use them in healthcare, finance and education, to name but a few. Without numbers, it would be much more difficult to understand trends and make important decisions, such as where the government needs to spend more money.

It would be wrong to think that statistics are just boring figures for nerds. They are the key to knowledge and progress. Huge amounts of data is collected on critical issues such as the environment, health and medicine and poverty. By analysing these numbers we can better understand and hopefully try to solve global problems.

I am also convinced that numbers and statistics have improved our daily lives. Everyday things like weather forecasts and online shopping are all driven by the numbers and statistics that are collected. And let's be honest, who doesn't love reading through the statistics on their own sporting activities? It's only possible thanks to numbers!

However, I do agree that there is an information overload nowadays, with everyone sharing everything on social media. I completely understand that some people feel like it is just too much. All the more important then, in a world of 24/7 news, opinions and trends, that we have numbers to help us make sense of everything.

Share

1 Before you read: Read the questions, then talk about your answers in class.

1. Do you do any of the following? Compare in class.
   › Use a tracker to count the number of steps you take per day or the number of calories you use. ‹
   › Check interest rates or share indexes online. ‹
   › Compare prices for goods or services online. ‹
2. The title of the article is 'Are we drowning in a sea of numbers'? What do you think this might mean?

2 While reading: Write one sentence summarising the main point made in each paragraph.

Professor James Roberts

1st paragraph: ______________________________

____

____

2nd paragraph: ______________________________

____

____

3rd paragraph: ______________________________

____

____

4th paragraph: ______________________________

____

____

Dr Emma Pearson

1st paragraph: ______________________________

____

____

2nd paragraph: ______________________________

____

____

3rd paragraph: ______________________________

____

____

4th paragraph: ______________________________

____

____

3 Add one more point of your own supporting each person's point of view.

YES: ____

NO: ____

4 Class discussion. Follow the instructions and discuss the statement: 'Today's world is too strongly number-driven.'

1. Divide the class into two groups, A and B. Group A agrees with the statement. Group B disagrees.
2. Collect points in favour of your group's position. Refer back to the article and to your answers to tasks 2 and 3.
3. Consider points the other group might come up with. Find arguments to counter these. Refer back to the article and to your answers to tasks 2 or 3 for ideas.
4. Have a discussion in class. Make sure everyone has the chance to speak.

5 Your view. Write a short article (around 200 words) for a company newsletter expressing your point of view on the dangers and benefits of numbers and statistics in the world today.

BALANCING WORK AND WELLNESS

In a world where approximately 70% of the working population works between 30 and 40 hours a week, achieving a balance between a demanding career and personal well-being becomes a significant challenge. It can be a real balancing act to manage time and look after your physical and mental health. However, there are ways in which we can incorporate sports, fitness and wellness into a busy schedule.

© Olutcti Alitiam

Start the day right: a 20-minute morning jog can increase cardiovascular efficiency by around 15%. If jogging is not your thing, then even a 15-minute brisk walk can increase energy levels and improve your mood, setting a positive tone for the rest of the day. What's more, research indicates that about 30% of highly successful individuals start their day with physical exercise!

Active commuting: Statistics show that 40% of people who cycle or walk to work report lower stress levels compared to those who commute by car. If your workplace is within a 5-mile radius, cycling can add up to 150 minutes of moderate aerobic activity per week. Which just happens to be the amount experts say we need to stay healthy! On top of that, leaving the car at home can reduce the carbon footprint by 5% per individual.

Desk-based fitness: Around half of the working population spends approximately 6 hours a day sitting at a desk. Introducing simple exercises like 5-minute stretching sessions every hour can reduce associated health risks significantly. These activities can also boost mental alertness and productivity by up to 15%. A recent report showed that standing desks can reduce back pain by 32% and increase energy expenditure by 50 calories per hour.

Active weekends: Around 55% of health-conscious individuals engage in weekend sports or activities. Participating in an hour of swimming, two hours of hiking or a 90-minute dance class can burn approximately 300 to 600 calories, depending on intensity. And these activities not only promote your physical health, they also enhance social interactions and mental relaxation, cutting down stress levels by 40%.

Mindfulness and meditation: Spending just 10-15 minutes a day doing some form of meditation or mindfulness activity can lead to a 25% reduction in stress and a 20% increase in focus. A recent survey showed that 38% of top executives use these kind of activities to boost their mental well-being and deal with stress. Making time to end the day with a calming exercise can also improve sleep quality by 35% and reduce symptoms of anxiety and depression by 30%.

Of course, nobody is perfect and sometimes life just gets in the way of good intentions. However, as these examples show, sometimes even a little effort can make all the difference.

Share

1 Before you read: Discuss these questions in class.

1. Approximately what percentage of your time is taken up by work and family? How much time do you have left for sports, wellness activities or hobbies? And how do you measure your fitness (mobile phone, smart watch, etc.)?
2. How satisfied are you with your current work-life balance?

2 Read the text and find at least two benefits for each of the following. Answer in your own words, not copying from the article.

1. going jogging or going for a walk in the morning
   a) ______________________________
   b) ______________________________
2. cycling or walking to work
   a) ______________________________
   b) ______________________________
3. exercising every hour at work
   a) ______________________________
   b) ______________________________
4. going swimming or hiking at weekends
   a) ______________________________
   b) ______________________________
5. meditating for a quarter of an hour a day
   a) ______________________________
   b) ______________________________

3 Focus on words: Find the expressions in the article which match these explanations. Then create a sentence relevant to your life using each expression. Share your sentences in class.

1. a job which is very stressful
2. an attempt to manage a number of different obligations at the same time
3. a very full timetable
4. be something you like doing
5. which by chance is …
6. in addition to this
7. the rate at which people perform and / or products are made
8. be a deciding factor in improving a situation

4 Chat with a partner: Which of the tips given in the article do you already follow? And which would you be most and least likely to follow? Explain why.

5 Class discussion. Follow the instructions and discuss this question in class. 'Should companies do more to improve the mental and physical health of their employees, or is this something everyone is individually responsible for?'

1. Collect points in favour of your position. Refer back to the article and to your answers to task 2.
2. Consider points people with an opposing view might come up with. Find arguments to counter these.
3. Have a discussion in class. Make sure everyone has the chance to speak.

› p. 29 in digital module 1.1.C

Final Milestone

START
of your project

What can you say or ask someone to find out how to say their name?

Step 1

Say a word or phrase that means …
a) be more than happy to
b) apparently
c) in retrospect

Step 2

Explain the difference between Miss, Mrs and Ms.

Step 3

Find at least six different ways of greeting someone in writing.
If you can, you can all move 1 square forward. If you can't, you must all move 1 square back.

TEAM TASK

Say three things about your job using the following expressions: *right now, usually, last month.* Make sure you use the correct form of the verb.

Step 4

Where do *since* and *for* go in the following statements?
I've worked there _____________ 5 years.
I've worked there _____________ 2005.

Step 5

What can you say to introduce someone to someone else?

Step 6

You're off sick.
Take a breather!
The team member to your right takes the next turn.

RELAX

Suggest four different phrases you can use to greet someone you meet again.

Step 7

Say three different things to end a meeting, a talk or a chat with someone.

Step 8

Say three things to …
a) avoid making a mistake with a name.
b) describe your job.
c) say goodbye to people you have visited.

MILESTONE A

How to play Play in pairs or fours. Use coins to play. Heads = Move one square. Tails = Move two squares. Complete the task on the square you are on. If you do it correctly, you can stay on the square, if you don't, you have to go back one square. If you are on a yellow square, the whole team, all the players, have to work together and do the task. If you get it right, each team member moves forward one square, if you don't, each team member moves back one square.

Say at least three different things in response to the following: *Are you free for a catch-up meeting on Friday?*

Step 9

What are three different ways to say that a suggested meeting time and day is possible for you.

Step 10

What's the hurry? - *Rome wasn't built in a day either!*
The team member to your right takes the next turn.

RELAX

How can you make these sentences sound less formal?
a) Please find … in the attachment.
b) I'm writing to ask …
c) The aim of the meeting is …

Step 11

In your own words, paraphrase what you say when you …
a) run through an agenda.
b) recap decisions.
c) establish rapport.

Step 12

What do you do when you hear:
a) Could I ask everyone to go on mute?
b) Would you please take the minutes today?

Step 13

Think of at least six different things to say or ask when progress reports are discussed in a meeting.

TEAM TASK

What do these abbreviations stand for?
a) AOB
b) tbc
c) asap

Step 14

Say *They make good progress.* using the passive voice in:
a) present progressive
b) simple past
c) future

Step 15

Compare online and face-to-face meetings. Think about:
a) efficiency and cost
b) ability to discuss
c) carbon footprint

Step 16

Find words with the opposite meanings to these words:
a) shy
b) introverted
c) silent

Step 17

Which three things can you say when you are …
a) moving from one topic to the next?
b) managing an online meeting?
c) comparing online and face-to-face meetings?

MILESTONE B

If you're on a green square, you don't have to do a task. The player to your right takes the next turn. Red squares are milestone squares. If you complete the task correctly, you can move forward two squares. If you don't, you stay on the square. The player to your right takes the next turn. The player who reaches the last red square of the game is the winner.

Finish these sentences.
a) Most days I / we …
b) At the moment I / we …
c) For the past year I / we …
d) Last month I / we …

Step 18

Talk for one minute about the organisation you work for. Give at least five different statistics.

Step 19

Say this time in three different ways:
6:30 am

Step 20

How can you say this sentence differently?
One in five employees works part time.

Step 21

You're on holiday -
Let your hair down a bit!
The team member to your right takes the next turn.

RELAX

Name three different types of charts to visualise changes in a company's market share.

Step 22

What can you say to describe the change in figures?
Sales were 3 million last year and are just over 4 million this year.

Step 23

Is it *rise* or *raise?*
a) She asked them to ________ her salary.
b) Costs will ________ steadily.
c) They will ________ their prices.

Step 24

Say three things from your work experience that go with each of the phrases below:
a) humble beginnings
b) a game changer
c) the sky's the limit

TEAM TASK

Find three ways of saying that becoming more profitable is your company's plan.
We ____________ become more profitable.

Step 25

Spend one minute talking about your plans and expectations for your next holiday.

Step 26

Say the following in three different ways:
a) nearly 1 million
b) numbers have declined
c) the aim is

MILESTONE C

Find out who in your team …
a) has made a mistake with someone's identity.
b) provides support.
c) is looking forward to something.

Step 27

Say three things you can do to …
a) make meetings more effective.
b) balance work and wellness better.
c) avoid misleading readers of statistics.

TEAM TASK

You want to greet someone by name. Say three things you need to think of first to greet them correctly.

Step 28

Say three things you say to start a meeting.

Step 29

What do these acronyms stand for?
a) CEO
b) CFO
c) IT Director

Step 30

What does *go along with something* mean? Give three different meanings.

Step 31

What do these words mean?
a) short-time work
b) timescale
c) a good number

Step 32

What do you say in response to *How do you do?*

Step 33

Say three things you say to close a meeting.

Step 34

No hurry! Your boss is still in a meeting. *Just take a chill pill.* You've almost made it. The team member to your right takes the next turn.

RELAX

Write about what you've done on your course in the style of the minutes of a business meeting (words and phrases, grammar, practice, talking, revsion, fun etc.).

Step 35

GREAT JOB!
You have successfully completed your project.

Personal greetings & responses

- Welcome to *[name of organisation]*.
  › Thank you for inviting me.
- A: How d'you do? › B: How d'you do? *(formal)*
- Good morning / afternoon / evening (everyone).
- Pleased / Nice / Delighted to meet you!
- It's a pleasure to meet you.
  › I can only say the same in return.
- It's great to be here / to finally meet you in person.
- It's good to put a face to a name at last.
- I've been looking forward to meeting you.

Introductions

- May I introduce myself (to anyone who doesn't know me yet)?
- Hello, my name's *[full name]*.
- I'm *[full name]* from *[organisation]*.
- Let me introduce you to *[name / position]* some colleagues. › Thanks, that's very kind of you.

Meeting again

- Good / Great / Nice to see you (again)!
- How are you?
- How's it going? / How are things? *(informal)*
- (I'm) Fine, / Very well, / Not so bad, thanks. And you?

Greeting a large group

- Good morning / afternoon / evening, everyone.
- Thank you all for coming.
- It's great to see so many familiar faces here today, as well as all the newcomers.
- Before we get down to business, may I introduce myself to anyone who doesn't know me yet?

Saying goodbye

- Goodbye! / Bye! / Bye for now!
- It was / It's been nice meeting you / talking to you.
- It's been a pleasure to get to know you.
- Have a safe journey / flight.
- Take care.
- See you again soon.

Showing interest in future contact

- We must keep in touch.
- Let's catch up again soon.
- I'll look / I look / I'm looking forward to seeing you.
- Keep me up to date (on …).
- Let me know if there's anything else I can do.

› Your phrase bank

› p. 30 in digital module 1.1.A

Opening a meeting

- Let's get started.
- Let's get down to business.
- Is everyone happy with the minutes of the last meeting?
- Can I just clarify the objective of today's meeting?
- The main aim of the meeting is to …
- So, let's kick things off.

Moving a topic on

- Sorry to cut you off but I don't think we have time to go into this now.
- We're running short on time.
- So, moving onto the next item.
- I think we've already covered this topic enough.
- We can come back to it later, if there's time (at the end).
- Can I hand over to you for this one / point / topic?
- So, the next point we need to cover is …

Reporting on progress

- Paul, can you update us?
- I have the latest … here.
- What's the latest on …?
- We've been making good progress.
- Progress has been a bit slow.
- Have we … yet?
- Not quite, but we're close to …
- Things are / aren't looking good / aren't looking too bad.
- Could you bring us up to speed on …?
- When do you estimate … will be ready?
- If all goes / If things go according to plan …,
- I'd guess it will be ready in a fortnight / by next month.

Closing a meeting

- I'm afraid that's all we have time for today.
- When's the next meeting?
- It's scheduled for …
- I'll send the minutes and action points round later today.
- Thank you all for coming today.
- Is everyone happy with the action points we've agreed (on)?
- Then let's bring this meeting to a close.

› Your phrase bank

› p. 30 in digital module 1.1.B

Useful questions

- When was the company founded?
- How many people are employed there?
- How big is the company?
- Has the company grown over the last ten years?
- Why have you decided to (raise prices)?
- How much will you be (raising prices by)?
- What kind of timescale are we talking about here?
- What are your goals moving forward?
- What effect has the economic crisis had on your company?

Reporting on development

- We're seeing steady growth.
- The company has grown over recent years.
- Our annual revenue rose to (almost $37 million last year).
- Costs have almost doubled.
- Turnover has risen / fallen by (€3.5 million).

Essential verbs

- to achieve a goal (within a certain time)
- to add
- to aim high
- to be founded (The company was founded in …)
- to double (Prices have doubled.)
- to expand
- to grow by (ten percent) / to increase by (ten percent)
- to pick up
- to raise (prices by …)
- to reduce
- to rise
- to see a reduction (in turnover)
- to see steady growth
- to start up (We started up in …)

Essential expressions

- a good number (That sounds like a good number to me.)
- a handful
- a small increase (in prices) / an increase by (ten percent)
- a third / a quarter / a fifth
- almost / around / approximately (I think around approximately 2,500.)
- at least
- over the next five years
- the exact number (I don't know the exact number.)
- Due to circumstances beyond our control.
- We had no choice in the matter.
- That's good news then!

› Your phrase bank

› p. 30 in digital module 1.1.C

Abbreviation: shortened form of a word or expression
Acronym / initialism: formed from the first letter of each word in a term
Acronym: often spoken as one word (e.g. PIN)
Initialism: each letter pronounced separately (e.g. AOB).
Some acronyms can be pronounced as words or as individual letters (e.g. VAT).
You can't find a term in the list? Just look it up in an online acronym finder.

a.m. (am) ante meridiem (before noon)
AI artificial intelligence
AIDA attention, interest, desire, action
AOB any other business (e.g. on an agenda)
approx. approximately
asap as soon as possible
B2B business-to-business
B2C business-to-consumer
BCC blind copied (email)
BST British standard time
BTW by the way
CC copy circulated (email); carbon copy
CDO chief data officer
CEO chief executive officer
CET central European time
corp. corporation
CRM customer relations / relationship manager
CSR corporate social responsibility
CTO chief technology officer
CV curriculum vitae
DM direct message, direct mail
e.g. exempli gratia (for example)
encl. enclosed
ETA estimated time of arrival
etc. etcetera (and so on) (spoken as a full word)
FAQ frequently asked question(s)
FYI for your information
GMT Greenwich mean time
HQ headquarters
HR human resources
i.e. id est (that is, in other words)
IMO in my opinion
IT information technology
KISS keep it short and simple
KPI key performance indicator
LLC limited liability company
Ltd. limited (spoken as a full word)
MD managing director (UK)
MNC multinational corporation / company
N/A not applicable
NGO non-governmental organisation
no. number
OOO / OOTO out of the office
p.a. per annum
pm post meridiem (after noon)
PA personal assistant
PIN personal identification number
PLC; plc public limited company (UK)
POC point of contact
pp paginae (pages); per procurationem
PPC pay per click
PTO please turn over (OR: paid time off)
R&D research and development
re with reference to; regarding
Re. reply (email)
Ref. reference
ROE return on equity
ROI return on investment
RSS really simple syndication
RSVP répondez s'il vous plaît (please reply)
SEO search engine optimisation
SME small to mid(-sized) enterprise (AE)
small to medium(-sized) enterprise (BE)
SMS short messaging service (text messaging)
sq. square
SWOT strengths, weaknesses, opportunities, threats
T&C terms & conditions
TBA to be announced
TBC to be confirmed
TBD to be decided
TED technology, entertainment, design
ToS terms of service; terms of sale
URL uniform resource locator
USP unique selling point; unique selling proposition
VAT value added tax
VP vice-president
VPN virtual private network
WFH working from home

› p. 31 in digital modules 1.1.A|B|C

approve *agree or accept, often officially*
arrange *organise or make plans*
attend *be present at a place or event*
benchmark *standard used for comparison*
big data *large volumes of data analysed for patterns and trends*
branding *creating a unique identity for a product or company*
budget *a plan of how much money you have and how you will spend it*
calculate *find a number or amount using mathematical methods*
capitalise *taking advantage of an opportunity*
client *a person or organisation that uses the services or advice of a professional or company*
cloud computing *storing and accessing data over the internet*
collaborate *work together on a project*
conduct *carry out or organise a task or activity*
confirm *verify or make sure something is true or accurate*
consider *think about carefully before making a decision*
contribute *give or add something, especially money or ideas, to help achieve a goal*
cooperate *work together towards a common goal*
customer *a person or organisation that buys goods or services from a business*
cybersecurity *protecting computers and data from unauthorised access*
data *information, especially facts or numbers, often used in business analysis*
deadline *the latest time something should be completed*
decision *a choice or judgment*
delegate *entrust a task or responsibility to someone else*
deliver *bring or provide goods, services or results*
depend *rely on or be influenced by something*
develop *grow or make progress*
diversity / diversify *variety of people, things or ideas within a group*
economy *the system by which a country's goods and services are produced and distributed*
efficient *being effective without wasting time or resources*
employee *a person working for a company or organisation*
encourage *inspire or support someone to do something*
evaluate *assess or judge the value or quality of something*
execute *carry out or perform a task or plan*
expand *increase in size, scope or importance*
feedback *information about reactions to a product, service or performance*
finance *the management of money and other assets*
forecast *predicting future events or trends*
goal *a specific objective or target*
growth *the process of increasing in size, quantity or degree*
guidance *advice or information provided to help someone make decisions*
handle *deal with or manage a situation*
implement *put a plan, decision or system into effect*
improve *make something better or enhance its quality*
inclusion *ensuring everyone feels welcome and valued*
income *money received, especially on a regular basis, for work or through investments*
inform *give information or make someone aware of something*
initiate *begin or start something*
innovate *introduce new methods or ideas*
inspect *examine or scrutinise something closely*
integrate *combining things or systems for effective operation*

› p. 32 in digital modules 1.1.A|B|C

invest *put money or resources into a business, project or activity*
issue *a topic or problem for discussion or debate*
lead *guide or direct a group of people or an organisation*
manage *be in charge of or control a situation, project or team*
market *the commercial environment in which goods and services are bought and sold*
monetise *making money from something*
negotiate *discuss and reach an agreement through compromise*
network *Interconnected computers / devices sharing resources*
objective *a specific goal or target to be achieved*
operate *function or work in a particular way*
opportunity *a favourable or advantageous circumstance or occasion*
optimise *making something as effective or efficient as possible*
organise *arrange or coordinate elements into a structured whole*
outcome *the result or consequence of a particular action or situation*
outsource *having work done by external parties*
participate *take part in an activity or event*
performance *the manner in which something or someone functions or operates*
policy *a set of principles or rules adopted by an organisation*
potential *the capacity for growth or development*
prioritise *arrange or deal with in order of importance*
process *a series of actions or steps taken to achieve a particular end*
product *an article or substance that is manufactured or refined for sale*
profit *a financial gain, especially the difference between revenue and expenses*
promote *encourage the popularity or success of something*
purchase *buy or acquire something*
recommend *suggest or endorse as being suitable or advisable*
record *a written or documented account of something*
recruit *find and hire new employees for a company*
reflect *think deeply or carefully about something*
regulate *control or manage according to a set of rules or standards*
relevant *closely connected or appropriate to the matter at hand*
remote working *working from a location other than a traditional office, using technology*
report *a formal account of the results or findings of an event or investigation*
research *the systematic investigation into and study of materials and sources*
resource *a stock or supply of assets that can be drawn upon when needed*
respond *reply or react to something*
review *assess or examine something again*
risk *the chance or possibility of danger, loss or injury*
salary *a fixed regular payment, typically paid on a monthly basis*
scale (up) *increasing size or scope to accommodate growth*
schedule *a plan that gives expected times for different things to happen*
strategic *relating to the identification of long-term goals and the means of achieving them*
streamline *simplifying a process for efficiency*
success *the accomplishment of an aim or purpose*
support *provide assistance, help or encouragement*
sustainable / sustainability *doing things without harming the environment or depleting resources*
target *an aim or goal towards which efforts are directed*
training *the action of teaching a person or group of people a particular skill*
turnover *rate of employee replacement*
workflow *sequence of tasks in a process or job*

› p. 33 in digital modules 1.1.A|B|C

› Module A – Session 1

2a A.01

Receptionist	Good morning, how may I help you?
Tanja	Hello, my name's Tanja Whittindale. I have an appointment with Nicola Garofalo.
Receptionist	Just a moment… . Tanja Whittindale … Ah, yes. I have your name here. Welcome to Garofalo Solutions, Tanja!
Tanja	Thank you.
Receptionist	OK, I'll just give you your badge. You'll need to wear it at all times while you're in the building.
Tanja	Thanks. Oh, actually, that's not how I spell my name. It's Tanja with a 'J', not a 'Y'.
Receptionist	Oh, yes, that's a mistake. Sorry about that.
Tanja	My surname is spelt wrong, too, and I'm not a 'Mrs' – if anything I'm a 'Ms'.
Receptionist	I'm terribly sorry, Tanja. I'll print out a new badge for you and leave out the title, if that's OK with you.
Tanja	That's great! Thanks. But - er - will it take long? I'm meeting Nicola at ten o'clock. I don't want to be late for my appointment with her.
Receptionist	Er, actually, Nicola is a he, not a she.
Tanja	Oops! Thanks for telling me. I thought …
Receptionist	Don't worry about it. You're not the first one to make that mistake! Anyway, I'll only be a couple of minutes, if you don't mind waiting. So, could you just spell your surname for me, please?
Tanja	Yes, W-H-I-T-T-I-N-D-A-L-E.
Receptionist	Thanks. And the other details – are they correct?
Tanja	Yes, Event Manager, Blue Sky Events.
Receptionist	Thank you. Right, I'll just go and do it now. If you'd like to take a seat in the waiting area, Tanja. Oh, and please help yourself to tea or coffee.

6b |1 A.02

Andy	Hi guys, this is Ghislaine Guillaume. She's visiting us from Canada.
Siobhan	Hello, pleased to meet you, Gillian. I'm sorry, I didn't quite catch your surname.
Ghislaine	It's Guillaume, but please call me Ghislaine.
Siobhan	Ah, Ghislaine, not Gillian. It's a French name, isn't it?
Ghislaine	Yes, but in some parts of France they pronounce it as Ghislaine. In Canada it's Ghislaine.

|2 A.03

Ghislaine	And your name is …?
Siobhan	I'm Siobhan, Siobhan Coughlan.
Ghislaine	Siobhan? Is that an Irish name?
Siobhan	Yes, it means "God's grace".
Ghislaine	Oh, that's interesting. And what did you say your surname was? I didn't quite catch it.
Siobhan	Coughlan. Look it's written here on my badge.
Ghislaine	Ah, Dr Coughlan. I'm so sorry. Have I pronounced it correctly?
Siobhan	Yes, but please call me Siobhan!

|3 A.04

Andy	Excuse me, I'm looking for a Mr Constantine Phoenix.
Phoenix	Hello? That's me. But I'm Phoenix Constantine and I'm not a Mr!
Andy	Oh, sorry. Someone found your badge in the lobby. I do apologise!
Phoenix	No problem! It happens all the time!
Andy	So, um, how do you prefer to be addressed?
Phoenix	Well, it's actually Mrs Constantine, but I'm happy with Phoenix.

|4 A.05

Andy	Well, pleased to meet you, Phoenix.
Phoenix	And you are …? Oh, I see from your badge that your name is … I'm sorry, but I'm afraid I have no idea how to pronounce your name.

Andy Nguyễn Xuân Phúc. It's a Vietnamese name.
Phoenix Nguyễn … have I pronounced it correctly?
Andy Yes, actually Nguyễn is my family name and, well, it's a bit complicated. Everyone calls me Andy.
Phoenix Andy! Lovely to meet you. Anyway, thanks again for the badge. Maybe we can catch up later.

› Module A – Session 2

3b A.06

Lisa Hello, I'm Lisa. I'm director of Human Resources at the local hospital. Nice to meet you!
Mike Hi, Lisa. Pleased to meet you too! I'm Mike, IT Manager at Titan Solutions.
Jeff Hi, everyone, I'm Jeff.
Lisa Hi, Jeff. So, what company do you work for?
Jeff Actually, I'm self-employed, as a key account management specialist in the wine sector.
Lisa Really, I've never heard of that before! What does that involve?
Jeff Well, I haven't been doing it for long, so right now I'm looking for potential new clients. Basically, I improve my clients' turnover!
Lisa Ah, so you're an accountant!
Jeff No, key accounts, that means key clients or customers. It's confusing, I know.
Lisa Yes, but I think I get it.
Jeff Actually, I have clients and customers. My clients are the ones who sell the wine, the vendors, and I advise them on the best marketing strategies. But I also analyse potential new customers, the ones who buy the wine from my clients. I build up and sustain strong relationships with my clients and their customers. And, in the process, I get to travel to wine regions and taste wines!
Mike Sounds wonderful! How long have you been doing it then?
Jeff I've just started, actually. I used to be a nurse, but I decided to quit last year.
Lisa Oh, why was that?
Jeff It's a tough job, as you can imagine. Rewarding, yes, but the pay wasn't great. And I've always been interested in wine, so I decided to give it a try. I got the idea from a friend who runs a vineyard! I gave him advice on how to increase his sales, and things took off from there. Anyway, what about you, Mike? You're an IT manager, aren't you?
Mike Yeah! I manage a team of sixteen people. And basically, we do everything – we provide technical support and make sure the computer systems run smoothly. All that kind of thing. It's very varied. There's no day like the next!
Jeff Do you do a lot of troubleshooting?
Mike Yeah, that can be pretty demanding on a day-to-day basis. I'm also responsible for the IT budget, and I oversee data security. That's an important part of my job. It can be very challenging too.
Lisa Is security a big concern?
Mike Yeah, it is. At the moment we're developing a new cybersecurity system to protect our network. Obviously, I can't give any details! So, anyway, how about you, Lisa? How long have you been working in Human Resources?
Lisa Me? Oh, I've been in HR since I left college. I worked my way up through quite a few companies, then I worked as a Personnel Manager for an engineering company for five years, then two years ago I joined the hospital in my current role.
Mike Is working in a hospital very different from your work at the engineering company?
Lisa Not really. Both are very interesting. The main difference is that now I'm in the public sector, where our focus is on people, not profit. But the job responsibilities are similar, recruiting staff, organising training, and so on. In fact, we've just started a major new recruitment drive. We're trying to attract nurses who have retired, or who have left for other reasons. So, if you're thinking of coming back to nursing, just give me a call!
Jeff Thanks, but no, thanks! I'm very happy doing what I'm doing!

› Module A – Session 3

2a |1 A.07

Iris Hi Anika, I'd like you to meet Lorenzo Valenta. Lorenzo is head of sales at our headquarters in Barcelona. He's here for the sales conference. Lorenzo, this is Anika Benz. She's the new team leader in the production department.

Lorenzo Hello Anika, nice to meet you!

Anika How d'you do, Lorenzo. I've been looking forward to meeting you in person.

|2 A.08

Iris Good morning, Mr Fischer. Please allow me to introduce you to Lorenzo Valenta, Head of Sales at our headquarters in Barcelona. Lorenzo, this is Mr Fischer, our CEO.

Mr F How d'you do?

Lorenzo How d'you do?

Mr F Delighted to meet you, Mr Valenta. I'll look forward to seeing you at the sales conference later on.

Lorenzo Thank you. I'm looking forward to getting to know everyone, too.

› Module A – Milestone

2a A.16

Andy Hi guys, this is Ghislaine Guillaume. She's visiting us from Canada.

Siobhan Hello, pleased to meet you, Gillian. I'm sorry, I didn't quite catch your surname.

Ghislaine It's Guillaume, but please call me Ghislaine.

Siobhan Ah, Ghislaine, not Gillian. It's a French name, isn't it?

Ghislaine Yes, but in some parts of France they pronounce it as Ghislaine. In Canada it's Ghislaine.

b A.17

Ghislaine And your name is …?

Siobhan I'm Siobhan, Siobhan Coughlan.

Ghislaine Siobhan? Is that an Irish name?

Siobhan Yes, it means "God's grace".

Ghislaine Oh, that's interesting. And what did you say your surname was? I didn't quite catch it.

Siobhan Coughlan. Look it's written here on my badge.

Ghislaine Ah, Dr Coughlan. I'm so sorry. Have I pronounced it correctly?

Siobhan Yes, but please call me Siobhan!

c A.18

Andy Excuse me, I'm looking for a Mr Constantine Phoenix.

Phoenix Hello? That's me. But I'm Phoenix Constantine and I'm not a Mr!

Andy Oh, sorry. Someone found your badge in the lobby. I do apologise!

Phoenix No problem! It happens all the time!

Andy So, um, how do you prefer to be addressed?

Phoenix Well, it's actually Mrs Constantine, but I'm happy with Phoenix.

d A.19

Andy Well, pleased to meet you, Phoenix.

Phoenix And you are…? Oh, I see from your badge that your name is…… I'm sorry, but I'm afraid I have no idea how to pronounce your name.

Andy Nguyễn Xuân Phúc. It's a Vietnamese name.

Phoenix Nguyễn… have I pronounced it correctly?

Andy Yes, actually Nguyễn is my family name and, well, it's a bit complicated. Everyone calls me Andy.

Phoenix Andy! Lovely to meet you. Anyway, thanks again for the badge. Maybe we can catch up later.

› p. 36 in digital module 1.1.A

Module B – Session 1

2a B.01

Mia Hi, Tom. It's Mia here.
Tom Hi, Mia. How are you?
Mia I'm well thank you. I just wondered whether you're free to join a catch-up meeting on Wednesday at 2 pm to discuss the new automated chat system we are thinking of introducing?
Tom Let me check my calendar. I'm afraid I can't do Wednesday afternoon. But how about the morning instead? Or I'm also free on Thursday from 3 pm.
Mia Thursday from 3 would work well for me, actually. And we shouldn't need more than an hour,I don't think.
Tom Great! Are you thinking online or in person?
Mia I'd definitely prefer in person – unless that's a problem for you?
Tom No, no. That's fine. I'm in all day Thursday. Are you going to send a meeting request?
Mia Sure. And I'll include a draft agenda. Then you can add things if you need to.
Tom Perfect. Oh, and, is it just the two of us? Or who else will be attending?
Mia Good question. I'm thinking of asking Chris from IT and … whatshername – the new person from customer services – I can't remember her name off-hand.
Tom It's Helen Samuels, I think. Anyway, that sounds good to me. Looking forward to it.
Mia Great! See you Thursday then.
Tom Right. Oh and before you go, can I just ask you …

Module B – Session 2

4a B.02

Mia Right. It's 2 minutes past nine. Everyone should be here by now.
Tom Excuse me, Mia. Sorry to interrupt but Chris is in the waiting room.
Mia Ah, thank you. Hi Chris.
Chris Sorry, I was having trouble logging on.
Mia No, problem. OK, that's everyone here. So, let's go ahead and start. Welcome to the meeting everyone. Did you all get a copy of the agenda? Sorry, could I ask everyone to go on mute. If you could just use the thumbs up for a yes, raise hands icon to ask questions etc. It will make the meeting quicker. All right, then, let's get started. As you can see, we have several items today and I'd like to finish promptly by 11:30. So can I ask everyone to keep their inputs short.

5a B.03

Mia Sorry, Chris. I'm going to have to stop you there. I don't think we have time to go into so much detail now.
Chris Sorry, of course. I'll write it up in an email and send it to you all after the meeting.
Mia That would be great. Thank you. OK, so moving on to the next item on the agenda …

6a B.04

Mia So, just to recap on what we've said. We've agreed to work back from the chatbot launch date. Helen, you've agreed to arrange follow-up interviews with the focus group attendees in the next two weeks.
Helen Yes, that should be fine, but I think it might take 3 weeks.
Mia Sorry, I didn't quite catch that. I can't hear you very well with all the background noise.
Helen Sorry, is that any better?
Mia Yes, that's better.
Helen So, that should be fine, but I think it may take 3 weeks. I'll keep you up to date on my progress.
Mia Yes, please keep me posted. OK, I think we've covered everything for now. Let's schedule another meeting for next week. I'll email you the details later today. We'll have to finish there. Thanks everyone.

› p. 34 in digital module 1.1.B

› Module B – Session 3

4|1 ♫ B.05

Approval on minutes

Mia Right, let's get started. As usual, we have a lot to get through today and I'd like to finish promptly. So please keep on track and keep your inputs as short as possible. I'm assuming you've all read the minutes of the last meeting. Are there any objections? … No? Good. Then, I motion to approve the minutes. Who can second that?

Tom I second that.

Mia Thanks, Tom. So we can move on to the first point on the agenda now … Can I ask you all for a VERY short update on your action points from our last meeting.

|2 ♫ B.06

Update on action points

Mia Tom, could you update us on the findings from the new focus groups you ran, please?

Tom Sure. So, two new features of the chatbot were presented to the focus groups. The first one was a feature telling customers they were talking to a chatbot and not a person. Everyone really liked this feature. They liked the honesty. So, this feature will be added to the new version.

Mia Great! That sounds like a good idea. Were there any other points?

Tom Yes, they liked the new feature where they could choose to stop talking to the chatbot at any point and be connected to a real person.

Mia Won't everyone just choose to speak to a person? The idea of the chatbot is that it can deal with the simple enquiries and free up customer service people to deal with the harder queries.

Tom Yes, this is a concern. This needs to be monitored in the first weeks. It's a feature that might need to be changed.

|3 ♫ B.07

Latest chatbot update

Mia Have we got the latest version of the chatbot back yet?

Tom It is being sent later today.

Mia Have you seen any updates in between?

Tom I have. The 'personality' of the chatbot wasn't quite right. It was a bit too formal. I've asked for it to be changed to make it more friendly.

Mia That sounds hard to do.

Tom No, it's quite easy. The developers have several different 'personalities' they can change it to quite easily. The new personality will be supplied in the new version this afternoon.

Mia OK. Great! Let's hope it's more friendly.

|4 ♫ B.08

AOB / Matters arising

Mia Helen, do you know if everyone's holiday requests have been approved?

Helen There is one clash that is being discussed but all other holiday requests have been approved.

Mia Great! And have we decided who is going to represent us at the FDL conference?

Helen Yes, we have. We will be represented by myself and Tom. If anyone else feels they need to attend, please contact me as soon as possible so we can have rooms and things booked.

Mia OK, great. I think that's everything for today. Has a room been booked for the next meeting?

Helen No, it will be booked later today, and information sent round with the minutes.

› p. 35 in digital module 1.1.B

5b B.09

Interviewer In today's podcast we're talking to Jeremy Miles about face-to-face and online meetings. Jeremy, what's your view? Which kind of meeting is more effective in your opinion?

Jeremy There's not a definitive answer on that. Both have their advantages and disadvantages.

Interviewer OK. Then let's consider online meetings first.

Jeremy Right. Well, there are a number of obvious advantages to online meetings. They tend to be much more cost efficient than face-to-face meetings simply because face-to-face meetings require people to travel to one location. This involves travel costs and can involve hotel costs. Meaning face-to-face meetings are nearly always more expensive, before the meeting even gets started. And it's not just about money: Online meetings tend to be much more time efficient, because people don't need to waste time travelling to the meeting. People might not be able to do any 'real' work for a day just because of the time spent travelling.

Interviewer Yeah. That makes sense. Not to mention the carbon footprint involved, especially if you have to travel by plane!

Jeremy Absolutely! Travelling has a huge negative environmental impact. If you have 6 people all travelling for a meeting, then the carbon footprint is pretty high. Most companies these days are desperately looking to reduce their carbon footprint and online meetings are an easy way for this goal to be achieved. And lastly, face-to-face meetings tend to be more difficult to schedule than online meetings. When people attend a face-to-face meeting, you often need to find a whole morning or even a whole day when everyone is free. This is usually because of the time spent travelling. For online meetings, you just need to find one or two hours where everyone is free, and this increases the flexibility considerably – however it can also lead to meetings overload.

Interviewer Ah – what do you mean by that?

Jeremy Because it's so easy to organise an online meeting, there is a tendency to have more meetings and invite more people – without really thinking about what's necessary.

5c B.10

Jeremy Because it's so easy to organise an online meeting, there is a tendency to have more meetings and invite more people – without really thinking about what's necessary.

Interviewer. I see what you mean. So face-to-face meetings do have some advantages?

Jeremy Definitely. There are still clearly some advantages to face-to-face meetings. It is much easier for everyone to be really active. In an online meeting, turn taking can be much harder. In face-to-face meetings it is much easier for everyone to have an equal say and make themselves heard. Face-to-face meetings are also very important for team building – both at the meeting and before and after. There is the chance to have a coffee break or lunch together and this can be really positive for improving relationships in a team.

Lastly, face-to-face meetings often allow for more spontaneous discussions. Useful conversations can happen about topics that are not on the agenda. This rarely happens in online meetings, which tend to follow the agenda far more strictly.

Interviewer Right. Well, thanks Jeremy. Our time's nearly up now. So just one more question: Given the choice – which kind of meeting would you choose to attend?

Jeremy Hmm. That's a hard one! Online for routine discussions. But definitely face-to-face for important issues, kick-off meetings and where controversial topics are going to be discussed

Interviewer Thanks a lot for being with us today!

› Module B – Milestone

2
B.18

… Welcome to this week's episode of 'Working from Home' Today I'm going to talk about online meetings. While some say: "Yes, please!" and can't get enough of them, others are increasingly fed up with any form of digital collaboration. Well, virtual meetings offer significant benefits and drawbacks. First of all, online meetings reduce travel and accommodation costs. They are also very time-efficient, saving oneself the commute back and forth. Naturally, this results in a lower carbon footprint as studies have shown. However, these meetings can lead to more meetings than necessary, potentially decreasing overall productivity. Additionally, the virtual format may limit spontaneous discussions. Despite their efficiency, online meetings pose challenges in maintaining effective and engaging communication. I have invited an expert on the …

› p. 37 in digital module 1.1.B

› Module C – Session 1

3a C.01

Ellie Good morning and welcome to the latest episode of the Business Impact podcast. My name is Ellie James and today I am joined by Leah Billingham, co-founder of GreenFit, a leading producer of sustainable sportswear and equipment who are looking to take on the big boys on the international scene. Leah, welcome to the show.

Leah Thanks a lot, great to be here.

Ellie Well, let's start at the beginning. When did you start the company and what was your inspiration?

Leah Well, I started GreenFit back in 2007, with my partner Gareth. What was our inspiration? It was actually quite simple, really. When Gareth and I met at university, we were both really into sports and environmental issues. I knew early on that I wanted to either work in sports somehow, or do something in the area of sustainability, but I didn't think I'd get the chance to combine the two. But when the idea came to design sustainable sportswear, it just made sense, so we did some market research, worked on some designs, and the rest is history.

Ellie So what would you say your mission was when you started?

Leah Our mission was, and still is, to empower athletes of all abilities to achieve their goals while contributing to a healthier and more sustainable planet. As I said, we originally connected over sports and the environment, and we wanted to make this our goal.

Ellie Well, since those early days the company has grown into an international brand. You now employ approximately 4,400 employees worldwide, including 400 in your headquarters in Manchester. Tell us about this growth.

Leah It all went so fast. We found that our products were really sought after and to be honest, the hardest thing was trying to keep up with demand and building a creative and effective team of employees at the same time. Gareth and I decided to set up here in Manchester and go from there. We started with a small team and a limited product range as we concentrated on defining our identity and building the brand image. Gradually we added new products, more employees and slowly ramped up production. The next step was then to expand into new countries and markets.

Ellie Now, a little over 15 years later GreenFit has a portfolio of over 700 different products, including athletic apparel, footwear, accessories, and equipment for various sports disciplines from triathlon to Taekwondo, all sold in 313 retail outlets around the world.

Leah Actually, it's 314. We opened a store in Amsterdam just last week.

Ellie OK, 314. Well, however many it is, it's very impressive. And of course, there is a lot of logistics involved, particularly when you are so focused on sustainability.

Leah Absolutely. We want our products to have a limited carbon footprint, so we have eight production and logistic sites, strategically located to ensure sustainable production and shipping practices. On top of that, we have opened subsidiaries in 14 countries, enabling localised production under fair conditions, customer support and shorter shipping routes.

Ellie One of your main marketing channels is through sponsorship. In fact, I read that GreenFit sponsors over 60 professional and amateur sports teams.

Leah Sponsorship is nothing new for sports brands, but it was important for us to also be involved with female and disabled teams, and youth teams, so that we could contribute to the development of sports at all levels.

Ellie You recently published your financial figures for the last year and annual sales exceeded €1.3 billion, so it seems you are doing something right.

Leah We certainly hope so.

Ellie OK, let's take a short break now and listen to a short message from our sponsor. Afterwards, we will talk about the company's current projects.

› p. 34 in digital module 1.1.C

› Module C – Session 2

5a |1 C.02 As you can see on this pie chart, bills and expenses dominate the average household budget, accounting for 35% of the money available – that's the biggest light blue segment. Food expenses take up 25% of the budget (orange), transportation 20% (grey), healthcare and entertainment 10% each (yellow and blue respectively).

|2 C.03 As shown clearly in the bar chart here, the number of gym memberships decreased dramatically in March and only rose again in the summer, before falling in the autumn and winter.

|3 C.04 As you can see, the value of the shares has shown a steady decline over the last six months.

|4 C.05 What you can see here is that petrol prices reached a peak before falling a little and then maintaining the same level.

|5 C.06 A recent survey showed that a normal working day consists of 40% working on core tasks, 30% meetings and collaboration, 20% emails and other communication, and 10% leisure.

|6 C.07 This chart represents the age distribution of employees in a company. The largest age group is 30-39, accounting for 35% of the workforce, followed by 40-49 at 25%, 20-29 at 25%, 50-59 at 10% and 5% over 60.

› Module C – Session 3

2a C.08

Ellie Welcome back to the Business Impact podcast. I'm Ellie James, and I'm here with Leah Billingham, co-founder of GreenFit, a company that has experienced remarkable growth over the years. Now, Leah, let's talk about the future. What are GreenFit's plans and goals moving forward?

Leah Thank you, Ellie. The future is an exciting journey for GreenFit. Our main goal is to establish our presence in the global market and continue our commitment to sustainability. We've set some ambitious targets for the coming years. For example, we want to expand. In the next five years, we aim to open 50 new retail outlets, bringing our total to 364 stores worldwide.

Ellie That's very ambitious. Can you tell us something about the numbers behind this growth?

Leah Absolutely. We estimate an investment of around €250 million. This investment will cover not only the new stores but also further development of our existing locations, to make sure they meet our sustainability standards. We're confident that this will contribute to a substantial revenue increase in the coming years.

Ellie Impressive numbers. What about your product range? Do you have plans for expanding that as well?

Leah Yes, we're constantly innovating and expanding our product range to appeal to a wide range of athletes. Over the next three years, we're planning to introduce 150 new products across various sports, and we are going to focus on some new sports, such as cross fit and sailing. We also plan to introduce new sustainable materials for our sportswear and improve our technology in sports equipment. Our research and development team is working tirelessly to make this a reality.

Ellie You mentioned sustainability. Can you share more about your plans in that area?

Leah As you know, sustainability has always been at the core of our mission and we are setting ambitious environmental targets. By 2025, we plan to reduce our overall carbon emissions by 40% across our production and logistics. Over the next few years we are going to switch to 100% renewable energy sources for our facilities. As well as that, we're also focused on minimising waste and improving our packaging materials. It will be a challenge, but I am confident we will succeed.

› p. 35 in digital module 1.1.C

Ellie That sounds very impressive, but I'm sure these changes will come at a cost.

Leah Yes, of course. Over the next five years, we are going to spend around €80 million on these sustainability initiatives. For us, this is not only a responsibility to the planet, but also an opportunity. More and more customers are looking for sustainable products in all areas of their lives and it's a key driver of our brand loyalty.

Ellie And what about your employee growth? Will you be expanding your team further?

Leah Yes, as we expand into new markets and develop our product range, we will need to hire more talent. We're planning to add between 400 and 500 employees to our workforce over the next three years. It is really important for us to find people that fit to the company, that share our values and passion for sustainability and sport. I just hope we will find the right people.

Ellie Leah, it's clear that GreenFit has ambitious goals and exciting plans for the future. We look forward to following your journey. Thanks for sharing all these details with us today.

Leah Thank you, Ellie. We're excited about what lies ahead, and we appreciate the opportunity to share our vision with your listeners.

› Module C – Milestone

1 C.15

ShipAI has delivered a stellar performance in the latest financial quarter. When an 18% increase in annual revenue became public, the company's share price almost doubled. Net profits have gone up sharply to reach €550 million. This quarter has been the 4th best in the company's history. ShipAI's net profit margin stood at a robust 17.5% and the number of its clients has grown by about two fifths. In a labour market where highly-skilled workers are increasingly rare; its workforce has expanded to a total of 3,000 employees with about one in five coming from underrepresented groups. Average salaries at ShipAI have risen by a third in the last 5 years. ShipAI is raising its dividend to 38 cents a share.

› p. 36 in digital module 1.1.C

The authors and publishers acknowledge the following sources of copyright material and are grateful for the permissions granted. While every effort has been made, it may not have always been possible to identify the sources of all the material used, or to trace all copyright holders. If any omissions are brought to our notice, we will be happy to include the appropriate acknowledgements on reprinting.

Images

U1 Getty Images (LightFieldStudios), München; **6.1** Getty Images (PeopleImages); **6.2** 123RF.com (benzoix), Nidderau; **6.3** Getty Images (Luis Alvarez); **6.4** 123RF.com (bbtreesubmissio); **6.5** 123RF.com (zurijeta); **6.6** 123RF.com (dglimages); **7** 123RF.com (violin); **8.1** 123RF.com (modustollens); **8.1, 13.2, 20.1, 35, 41.1, 46, 60, 66, 71** Getty Images (a-r-t-i-s-t); **8.3** Getty Images (Edwin Tan); **9** CartoonStock.com (Chris Wildt), Bath; **10** 123RF.com (romastudio); **12.1** 123RF.com (fizkes); **12.2** 123RF.com (fizkes); **12.3** 123RF.com (valeriylebedev); **12.4** 123RF.com (stylephotographs); **13.1** Getty Images (Caiaimage/ Martin Barraud); **15** 123RF.com (docian); **16.1** Getty Images (Luis Alvarez); **16.2** Getty Images (gerenme); **16.3** Getty Images (Prostock-Studio); **17** Getty Images (andresr); **18** 123RF.com (thelivephotos); **20.2** 123RF.com (mangostar); **20.3** Shutterstock (Anatoliy Karlyuk), New York; **20.4** 123RF.com (funfunphoto); **20.5** 123RF.com (fizkes); **20.6** 123RF.com (fizkes); **22** 123RF.com (rawpixel); **26** Getty Images (Liubomyr Vorona); **28.1** 123RF.com (mehaniq); **28.2** 123RF.com (romanzaiets); **28.3** Getty Images (JHVEPhoto); **32** Getty Images (Golden Sikorka); **33.1** Getty Images (Cecilie_Arcurs); **33.2** Getty Images (fizkes); **36, 37** Getty Images (ozgurdonmaz); **38.1** CartoonStock.com (Huw Aaron); **38.2** CartoonStock.com (Jim Naylor); **38.3** Shutterstock (PSai2108); **38.4** Getty Images (Creative Crop); **38.4** CartoonStock.com (Mike Seddon); **40.1** Getty Images (Ridofranz); **40.2** Getty Images (BraunS); **41.2** Getty Images (AndreyPopov); **44.1** CartoonStock.com (Leo Cullum); **44.2** CartoonStock.com (Mike Shapiro); **44.3** CartoonStock.com (John Caldwell); **48** Getty Images (robuart); **50** Getty Images (AndreyPopov); **52.1** 123RF.com (wrightstudio); **52.2** 123RF.com (dotshock); **52.3** 123RF.com (petrovichvadim); **54.1** Getty Images (Portra); **54.2** Getty Images (mapodile); **56** Getty Images (AndreyPopov); **58.1** Getty Images (lucadp); **58.2** Getty Images (georgeclerk); **58.3** Getty Images (art12321); **58.4** Getty Images (mikimad); **58.5** Getty Images (Lightboxx); **58.6** Getty Images (alxpin); **58.7** Getty Images (Boris Panov); **59** Getty Images (pixelfit); **61.1** 123RF.com (konstantinks); **61.2** 123RF.com (alexkava); **61.3** Getty Images (siraanamwong); **61.4** Getty Images (LvNL); **62** 123RF.com (peopleimages12); **64** 123RF.com (studioworkstock); **66.1** CartoonStock.com (Marty Bucella); **70.1** Getty Images (andresr); **70.2** Getty Images (Mikolette); **70.3** Getty Images (rdonar); **70.4** Getty Images (fizkes); **73** CartoonStock.com (Crowden Satz); **74.1** Getty Images (Ariel Skelley); **74.2** Getty Images (Morsa Images); **74.3** Getty Images (SDI Productions); **74.4** Getty Images (michaeljung); **76.1** 123RF.com (nateemee); **76.2** Getty Images (simonkr); **76.3** Getty Images (EmirMemedovski); **78** Getty Images (emojoez); **80.1** Getty Images (Maskot); **80.2** Getty Images (Maskot); **82.1** 123RF.com (rotorania); **82.2** Getty Images (FG Trade); **82.3** Getty Images (skynesher)

Audio recordings and mastering

Bauer Studios GmbH, Ludwigsburg